SO MUCH BETTER

Life-Changing Strategies to Develop Calm,
Confidence & Curiosity to Become Your
Own Inspiring Success Story

Cindy Tsai, MD

This book contains advice and information relating to health care. It is
intended to replace medical advice and should be used to supplement rat
than replace regular care by your doctor. It is recommended that you seek y
physician's advice before embarking on any medical program or treatme
All efforts have been made to ensure the accuracy of the information contai
in this book as of the date of publication. The publisher and the aut
disclaim liability for any medical outcomes that may occur as a result
applying the methods in this book. Any perceived slight of any individua
organization is purely unintentional.

For permission requests, please email the author at: hello@cindytsaimd.co

The Library of Congress has catalogued the hardcover edition:
Control Number 2022907140

Hardback ISBN: 979-8-9860759-1-4
E-book ISBN: 979-8-9860759-0-7
Paperback ISBN: 979-8-9860759-2-1
Audiobook ISBN: 979-8-9860759-3-8

DEDICATION

*To all my teachers and guides, thank you
for sharing your wisdom.*

*To all my students, thank you for trusting me to
support your journey.*

SPECIAL GIFT

Just to say thanks for buying my book, I want to offer you my FREE VIDEO TRAINING SERIES!

Discover the *quickest* way to escape your comfort zone and achieve your dreams.

Scan the following QR code to access NOW!

cindytsaimd.com/somuchbetterbookgift

PLUS all the other videos, exercises, and meditations included in this book.

Don't wait.

Say "YES" to becoming an inspiring success story!

TABLE OF CONTENTS

INTRODUCTION

"Success is no accident." —Pelé

Are you comfortable? Maybe you have a decent job, a circle of family and friends, some money, reasonable health, and life is pretty good overall. Perfect. Check. Check. Check.

Or maybe you're exhausted. You've been doing everything right but still feel like something is missing . . .

How would you rate your life on a scale of 1–10?

Many people who have done self-development work or attained some level of "success" would rate things at a 7–8. Because life is relatively good and probably could get a bit better, but is overall fine.

Now, what if your 8 was actually only a 2? This does *not* mean that you are not good enough and going backwards. But rather, instead of two more levels, there are actually eight more levels you can attain and experience. How amazing is that?

This book is an invitation to help you see what is possible.

As a lifelong perfectionist and high achiever, I know what it's like to work hard and go after what you want. But after years of strenuous medical training to become a board-certified physician, I also experienced exhaustion, resentment, and burnout. I checked all the boxes but I was unhappy. It was scary to admit. I thought I was doing the right thing and on the right path to success . . .

Now, I get it.

Many people wouldn't care. And that's totally fine. It's nice when life is comfortable. It's easy. You don't have to worry about anything. If things are working, why fix them?

By the way, this book is not for people who don't feel stressed at all or have life "all figured out." I'm really glad to hear you are doing well and sending you all my best!

But if you are feeling a tiny nagging inside you to explore and wonder— (Because you know you have more in you. You know you have so much potential, if only you knew what to do!)—and you're curious about how things could be different . . . This book is for you.

Do you know what it's like to live life *all in*? And have things work out exactly as you wish? It's *not* too good to be true.

I want you to win. I want to help you become an inspiring success story. I want you to experience all the love, beauty, and joy in the world. Which of course means you will also have the hatred, ugliness, and sadness. No toxic positivity here. Life is not just rainbows and butterflies. You don't have to hide or disguise how you really feel. But I will teach you how to reprogram your brain's default and to become unstoppable.

When you can feel the lows, the highs become so much sweeter. So much better. You are alive. Connected to your *why*, to who you truly are. You're excited to wake up and can't wait to start your day. You are living your life's purpose.

Which means . . . You're not on autopilot. You're not wasting your time. You're not being complacent. You're not bored. You're not feeling drained before the the first meeting of the day. You're not unfulfilled. You're not constantly staring at the meeting room clock, swearing the second hand moves slower than the one on your clock at home. You're not distracted counting down the days till your next vacation getaway.

You are living on the next level. Fulfilling your true potential. This is what I hope for you.

HINT: In order to enjoy life, you have to be present.

You have to pay attention to what's going on. You have to be willing to see what's working and what's not. You have to be open to being uncomfortable. You have to be willing to say what you don't want to say and do what you don't want to do. Be brave enough to take a risk and stand in your truth. For the chance that life could get so much better.

I am beyond excited to share my Inspiring Success Story Method™ in this book, which has worked for many of my clients and will most likely support your journey as well.

I hate work. It's exhausting. What is this all for, anyway? But I feel bad. I've been so fortunate. I should be grateful. There are so many people out there who would love this life. So it isn't really that bad, right? Ugh. Just keep going. At least I have a vacation coming up in three weeks!

This narrative went on in my head for many years. I was embarrassed to share it. I was afraid of being judged. Because I did have a lot. I was lucky. I was educated. My parents worked hard to ensure I had a stable upbringing.

But I was unhappy. I felt like I was just going through the motions. I didn't see my value as a person and believed I could be easily replaced. I became resentful. I committed so many years of my life to becoming a physician. A lot of which was to make my Taiwanese parents proud.

When I think about it, I always felt like an outsider. I'm the youngest of four daughters with a big age gap in between, and my parents didn't plan to have me. Growing up, I told myself I was an accident. This recurring thought made me want to achieve and accomplish. To prove my worth. To show that my parents didn't make a mistake bringing me into the world.

So I worked really hard. Went to top schools (Johns Hopkins and Dartmouth). You don't just *stumble* into medical school and become a doctor. I studied, interviewed, took way too many exams to remember . . . I actively sought out opportunities, accolades, and accomplishments. All types of external validation. Just to fill a void inside myself.

I was relieved when I finally completed medical training in internal medicine and started working. I thought I could finally relax and live with ease. But it didn't work out that way.

While it was a privilege to serve as a primary care physician and medical director, I saw the impacts of chronic stress on the body. I was frustrated when patients came in with physical pains and ailments that stemmed from other areas of their life they weren't paying attention to. Patients often rushed in and out of my office, simply to check it off their to-do list before moving onto the next thing.

In this day and age, who *isn't* on autopilot?

I noticed that while people may experience different symptoms, disease often stems from a common root cause of inflammation. Stress is one of the most common ways to increase inflammation through the release of certain chemicals in the body. So I wanted to offer healing on a deeper level, addressing the root cause instead of covering up the symptoms. I wanted to

more than just prescribe medications as a Band-Aid. But I just didn't know
what else I could help.

kept going. I was on autopilot for so long.

didn't want to stop because I thought stopping meant something was wrong.
Stopping meant I would have to look at the reality. Stopping meant I would
have to recognize and admit to my real feelings: that I was unhappy. That I
was lost. That I was dissatisfied. That I was bored. That I was tired. That I
was unfulfilled. That I was wasting my precious years away doing something
I didn't really want to do.

I had to stop. My body forced me to.

woke up one day and I suddenly couldn't see. My eyes were blurry. I put on
my glasses. Wiped them three times. Still couldn't see. I put in my contacts.
Fresh new contacts. Still couldn't see. It was odd. Like the world I knew was
going away. I was terrified.

Our eyes guide us to where we need to go, after all. I was able to make an
urgent appointment and found that my prescription had worsened four times
overnight. Odd. There is a history of diabetes in my family, so the doctors
wanted me to get labs done to check if I was a new diabetic. As I got my labs
drawn and waited for results, all I could think was, *If only I didn't eat that piece
of cake or candy. If only I exercised more. If only I ate more veggies. If only this, if
only that.*

went to see a specialist who ran comprehensive tests on me. Used special
machines to look inside the back of my eye. And finally we had an answer.

was diagnosed with an autoimmune eye condition. One that could lead to
full vision loss. We needed to start treatment right away. I agreed. I didn't
have a choice. I knew my body was hurting and I had to listen. Steroids,
immunosuppressants, all the serious meds piled on one after another. I had

never liked taking meds, but I agreed. I wanted to get better. It sucks to [...] sick. I assembled a team for myself. I looked into healers and other speciali[...]

From the Western medicine perspective, an autoimmune disease is sim[...] when your own cells attack you. From an energetic/spiritual/East[...] perspective, I learned that autoimmune disease happens when you [...] rejecting yourself. The symbolism was stark. Deep down, I knew I had be[...] rejecting myself. I had lost connection with who I really was. And I ha[...] decision to make.

Did I want to stay the same? Or was I willing to do the work to heal and m[...] forward?

I wish I could say it was a breeze. That it happened overnight. Our societ[...] conditioned to value a quick fix, after all. But it wasn't. It was a process. A[...] it's constantly evolving and ongoing.

This work never ends. It's like an onion: As you peel one layer, you unco[...] another layer waiting for you. Or think about a fun rainbow or mille cr[...] cake, if you don't like onions.

So, this book is my gift to you. I'm sharing the various tools and resources t[...] have saved me in my healing journey. I have spent a lot of time, energy, a[...] resources learning and working from the best teachers, healers, and coache[...]

My friends and family know that I have always been interested in self-h[...] and self-development. And I continue to invest in various programs a[...] trainings. Not because I need to or have to, but because I want to and cho[...] to keep growing and feeling amazing. And I can't wait to share it all with y[...] in the simplest and most effective manner, a.k.a. this book. *(You're welcom[...]*

My hope is that you will be open to trying and exploring. Whether you're [...] or nearing burnout, or things are generally pretty good. I *want* you to be w[...]

Because only when you're well can you do your most important work in life—sharing your gifts and making the world a better place.

So often, we choose our life path early on and we never pause to reassess. It's like we make a decision and we don't let ourselves change our minds.

The reality is, things change. Life happens. Stress is a normal part of life. But when it becomes chronic and intense, it has detrimental effects on the body.

As a physician, I heard many stories from people in all walks of life. I became a doctor because I wanted to help people feel better. Not to prescribe pills that they would be dependent on for the rest of their lives.

In my own healing journey, I started exploring other ways of healing and came across the field of integrative medicine. This is where you put the patient at the center of their care and incorporate the best from both conventional and unconventional/alternative therapies. I'm happy to share that there are more evidenced-based studies coming out every day, and patient testimonials that make your heart warm and fill you with joy.

I always say, "Everyone is different, so the things you need are going to be different." We can't use a cookie-cutter approach.

The problem is, you won't know what works unless you try. We all wish we had the questions (or answers!) before going in to take the test, right? We want to know what will work but don't want to put in the work to figure it out. This is normal. It happens to everyone, myself included.

In particular, this book is for those of you who are feeling stressed and unfulfilled. For the high achievers who are ready to have more in their lives. For those who want to reconnect with who they really are. I will share a different perspective on stress management, take a comprehensive look at mind-body healing, and support your growth.

I'm going to teach you different tools and skills throughout the book so that you can start this journey for yourself. I have included various exercises, recordings, and videos for you because I want you to know that I'm right here with you. It's scary to do things alone, and I want you to know that you are never alone. Please reach out to me and let me know how things are going! I would love to support you along the way.

Now, onward!

To your *massive* success.

All my best,
Cindy

cindytsaimd.com
hello@cindytsaimd.com

HOW TO USE THIS BOOK

This book is meant to be a resource filled with practical tools and exercises to support your journey.

I have included numerous favorite tips and tricks that have worked for myself and so many of my clients.

I recommend proceeding from start to finish as organized to get the most out of this experience, as the contents build upon each other. I also encourage you to complete the exercises and resist the urge to skip them if you are serious about changing your life.

That being said, if you're eager to review a specific topic, feel free to jump ahead.

You can also always return to this book and reference certain sections depending on what's going on in your life at the time.

Remember that we may need different things at different stages in our lives. Visualization may not seem interesting to you right now but might become your favorite tool once you see how well it works for you.

My hope is that you will be open to identifying techniques and exercises that work best for you. Know that you don't have to apply everything all at once. If you have questions, email me (hello@cindytsaimd.com)—I'm here to help!

Information overload is one of the fastest ways to overwhelm, so don't try to rush and finish this book in one day. The key is integrating small bits and pieces over time to assemble your full masterpiece.

If you notice yourself getting tired, pause. Breathe. Feel your feet on the ground. Take a break.

Everyone finds happiness and fulfillment in their own way. Let's get judgment out of the way. No one is more or less successful. You get to write your own success story.

Lastly, if you are currently experiencing significant trauma or distress, please make sure to consult a healthcare professional. This book is *not* designed for deep trauma healing, and I want you to receive the best appropriate care.

You got this. Let's go.

PART I

SO WHAT?

What is this all for, anyway?

If you are one of those curious readers who like to investigate something before diving into it, the following pages will explain the essence of everything you need to know.

You will see why burnout happens, how to reset your brain's default, and the fundamentals of mindfulness to boost your well-being.

CHAPTER 1

THE PROBLEM

"No problem can be solved from the same level of consciousness that created it." —*Albert Einstein*

Before we start, I invite you to take a cleansing breath with me.

Inhale through the nose.

Pause.

Exhale through an open mouth and say "ahhhh." Feel the stress and tension leave your body.

Take a few more at your own pace.

Thank you for doing that. I hope you are feeling more grounded and present in this moment.

If you want to have more in your life, you have to retrain your system and learn how to calm your system down. By *system*, I mean your mind and your body.

Now, before we get into all the tools and tricks to get you more of what you want, it would be remiss if we didn't check in to make sure we're going in the right direction.

It's like you want to get to "Paradise" so you jump in your car, excited and ready to go. But as you start to type *P-A-R-A-D* in your GPS, you pause and ask yourself, *Where is that? What's the address?*

So before you jump into your car and waste your time and energy driving to nowhere, let's evaluate where you want to go.

It's easy to get caught up in the moment, start making checklists and signing up for courses, this and that. Wanting to get the *how* down. But I invite you to consider that you need to learn the *who* first, and then the *how* comes after. This means that you have to get clarity on who you need to be and then, from that place of knowing, the *how* becomes much easier because you already know.

So take a moment to pause and ask yourself *why* with these three questions.

1. Why am I doing what I'm doing?
2. What is my purpose in life?
3. Am I happy?

If you find yourself unable to come up with an answer, don't fret. So often, we don't take time to reflect and reconnect with who we really are.

One of the main skills I want to teach you is how to be kind to yourself, a.k.a. self-compassion. As I learned in my journey with autoimmune disease, when we are critical of ourselves, all that means is that we're rejecting ourselves. And no one can take the amount of criticism and negativity people like us tend to pile on ourselves. Nor should they.

Think about this: Is it easier for a kid to thrive in a home of praise or of judgment? I find that we are often quick to offer support and kindness to others but are conversely so hard on ourselves. We've been conditioned to think that we have to be hard on ourselves in order to keep moving forward. But research has shown that this is completely false.

As researcher Kristin Neff has shared in her book *Self-Compassion*, practicing self-compassion doesn't mean letting yourself off the hook. On the contrary, research from Breines et al. has shown that self-compassion leads to taking more responsibility for our actions. A recent meta-analysis study from Liao et al. also supports the idea that self-compassion enhances motivation and leads to higher self-efficacy, meaning you have more confidence in your ability to succeed.

I want you to know that everything you have and don't have in your life now is the culmination of all the things you've done up until this point.

We often use our past as a way to determine what's possible in the future. *I should be able to make X amount of money within this time frame because that's what I did last year . . .* Stop. That's not how it works. That's just your mind feeding you stories from the past.

If you are always using your past to determine what's possible in your future, how will you *ever* get more of what you want? How will you have a better and more extraordinary life?

Before we continue, I want you to first acknowledge yourself and all the hard work you've done. All the impressive achievements and accomplishments that you've attained to get to this point.

EXERCISE: CELEBRATE YOU

Take a moment to write out all the wins you had this week! Can you think of at least five? What went well? And once you're done writing them down, give yourself a pat on the back!

1. _____
2. _____
3. _____
4. _____
5. _____

How was the exercise for you? Was it easy? Hard?

If it was hard, ask your inner critic/judging self to take a break and leave you alone so you can try again. Or think about what a loved one would say to you about all of the wins you had this week!

Now the moment of truth . . . The reason you don't have what you want in life is because you don't yet believe it's possible (for you).

But this is good news, because it all starts with awareness.

HINT: We can't change what we don't know.

Because if you don't know something, how would you know what or that you even need to change? It's like you're always driving the same forty-minute route to get to your favorite coffee shop, not realizing there's a back-end shortcut that would take you ten minutes instead. But once you learn the shortcut, you wouldn't keep wasting your precious time going the long route anymore, right?

vite you to consider that you are in a safe bubble right now. Your zone of
iliarity, or comfort zone. But everything you really want is actually outside
his comfort zone. Sorry. It's true.

might think you need to work harder. To hustle! Pull an all-nighter!

the answer is *not* to try harder. You already work hard enough. In fact,
is exactly why burnout happens.

nout is a state of emotional, physical, and mental exhaustion caused by
essive and prolonged stress. We are so conditioned to stay in autopilot
de and keep going that we never pause to recalibrate and rebalance. We
e trained our system to be and remain in a chronic state of stress and
vival.

ve you heard of the one-in-sixty rule? Aviation experts have shown that for
ry one degree a plane veers off course, it misses its target destination by one
e for every sixty miles it flies. Doesn't seem like a lot, but it all adds up. If
are flying from JFK to LAX with just one degree off course, you're going
and in the Pacific Ocean instead of a beautiful warm patio looking out to
Malibu sunset and watching whales and dolphins roam freely.

longer you go without full awareness, the further you stray from your
tination.

en you make the mistake of trying too hard (especially when focusing on
wrong things), all that's doing is sending a sign that you *don't* have enough.
at you are incomplete and that there is a void inside.

ybe deep down you don't believe you are not good enough yet. Imposter
drome, anyone? And you have to keep seeking the answers outside yourself.

en that couldn't be further from the truth. I know we may not have
nally met, but I want you to know that . . .

You are *enough*. Right *now*. Just as you are. In this very moment.

Keep reading to learn how to make this your reality!

<u>QUESTIONS</u>

1. What is my *why*? What fuels me and lights me up? What am I here do?
2. Do I beat myself up? Am I open to being kind to myself instead?
3. What do I want that's outside my comfort zone?

CHAPTER 2

HOW THE BRAIN WORKS

"The body achieves what the mind believes." —*Napoleon Hill*

I want you to recognize that the mind and body are not separate. In order to have what you want, you need to help the mind and body work together cohesively like a well-oiled machine.

Have you ever felt like you get stuck or something comes up just when you're about to make a big breakthrough? Or do you hear yourself saying, "This always happens to me"? It's like you're a magnet that attracts all the *wrong* things. More stress. More anxiety. More struggle. Ugh. *No thank you.*

When your mind and body are in opposition, you will most likely not be as productive or impactful as you are meant to be. The process is learning how to leverage the mind-body connection so that you can be supported and successful in all your endeavors. Only then will you experience how easy everything really can be and ditch the hustle or struggle.

Now, every time we try to go after what we want, it's going to feel scary. As it should, because our system (mind and body) is worried that we're putting ourselves in danger. But the reality is that there's a difference between fear and danger.

Fear is a normal physiological response that happens when we encounter something new and unfamiliar. Danger, on the other hand, is a situation that can cause serious harm or injury.

When you want to change your life for the better through expressing yourself authentically, strengthening your boundaries, making a ton of money, or something else, this will trigger your fear response because it is unfamiliar. You will feel uncomfortable. But this is not a red light to stop.

In fact, you must learn how to love this fear and embrace discomfort so that you can grow and expand beyond your wildest dreams.

HINT: Fear is not the same as danger.

So how do you embrace the fear? You must learn to create safety in your own system. When your system is able to stay calm, the fear remains but no longer works against you and holds you back.

The human body is an elegant machine with many moving parts that coordinate to work together as seamlessly as they can. It contains different systems that have their own separate objectives under the overarching umbrella of "survival"—that is, each system has its own objective to keep us alive. So, I want you to start seeing everything your mind and body want you to do through the filter of "Is this going to promote survival?"

Depending on your past experiences, some events will be more shocking than others for you. If you grew up enjoying eating organ meats, trying pig intestine might not seem like a big deal to you. Conversely, if you haven't tried this before, the thought of eating an animal's digestive organ will probably not appeal to you, and may even bring a sense of disgust. Because it is unfamiliar, it will likely trigger the brain's survival instincts to veer you away.

I want you to remember that you are here on your own journey.

This journey is a process, meaning that it takes time for things to unfold. But before you get discouraged, I want to reassure you that it doesn't mean progress is going to be slow. It all depends on how committed you are to this process.

As you start down this path, you have to recognize that, biologically, the top priority of the mind and body is to keep you alive. Your body doesn't care that you want to make a million dollars or go on a vacation to the Maldives. It wants you to stay alive, right now.

And it does this by coordinating various body systems and helping them work together. We have the circulatory system, where the heart and blood vessels pump blood to bring nutrients and fuel to parts of the body. We have the digestive system, where the stomach, intestines, liver, and other organs break down and absorb nutrients to feed the body. We have the lymphatic system to fight off infections and keep us healthy. And so on. But I want to draw your attention to the nervous system in particular.

The brain communicates with the body using an internal messenger system called the autonomic nervous system. The nervous system is how the body responds to stress. It's the central command system, made up of the brain and nerves.

The nervous system is split into two main components or sides: the sympathetic (fight or flight) and parasympathetic (rest and digest). Both sides are connected to all of our internal organs, such as the heart, lungs, muscles, and so on. One side of the system will switch an organ on—like pressing the gas pedal—in order to help with survival, while the other side of the system will calm an organ down—like pressing the brake pedal—in order to carry out daily functions.

As an example, let's say you are walking all alone down a dark alley at night. Suddenly, you hear footsteps coming up behind you. Your brain registers that something scary might be going on. It turns on the sympathetic system, and then your heart rate increases, your palms get sweaty, and your muscles contract to help protect vital organs and prepare for fight or flight.

On the other hand, when you're at a spa, waiting to get an amazing massage, listening to calming music, sipping some chamomile tea, staring out to a beautiful mountain view . . . The brain notices how everything feels safe and reassuring. It turns on the parasympathetic system, leading to various relaxing responses in the body, such a slower heart rate and release of muscle tension.

You may have heard of the vagus nerve in particular, and that's the main nerve that regulates the parasympathetic system to help with the relaxation response. It connects your brain to many important organs in the body, including the stomach, heart, and lungs. A helpful skill is to learn how to activate the vagus nerve to turn on the parasympathetic system, so that your body can stay calm, instead of switching on the sympathetic system, which can in the long term lead to a chronic state of stress.

I'm going to get technical for a bit and let you know that the key is to develop vagal "tone." Vagal tone represents the activity of the vagus nerve. Having higher vagal tone means your body will relax faster after stress. Studies, including one from Breit et al., have shown that the more you increase your vagal tone, the more your physical and mental health will improve, and vice versa. Know that the vagal response reduces stress and helps your system relax.

I always like to remind people that stress in and of itself is not a bad thing. It's only when the stress is chronic that it can lead to detrimental effects like inflammation, chronic diseases, hormonal changes and imbalance, chronic pain, various health issues, and so on.

When you are under stress, your body turns on the sympathetic nervous system. This leads to your organs and systems working overtime and extra hard. Think about a race car driver pressing down on the gas pedal until the

end of a race to beat their competitor to the finish line. As you can
bably imagine, that is not sustainable. We have to take breaks periodically,
reset and rebalance, because we do not an infinite supply of energy. This
hy we need sleep and rest to recover and recuperate.

ow me to review the stress pathway and further explain the mind-body
nection so you can see where the opportunities are.

mentioned in the beginning of this chapter, the mind and body are not
ally separate, even though we often think they are.

ve you ever felt nauseous when you're anxious about something?
erienced butterflies in your stomach right before you had to speak in
lic? I know I have. That's actually one of the most common examples of
mind-body connection at work. When you are having anxious thoughts,
r body physically responds to them.

MIND-BODY CONNECTION
(HOW STRESS REALLY WORKS)

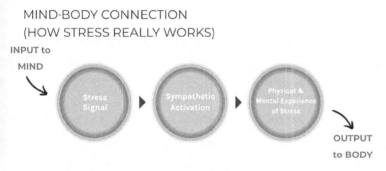

Figure 2.1: Mind-Body Connection/Stress Pathway

ou can see in Figure 2.1, starting at the left, input from the nervous system
ent to the mind, and the brain is constantly scanning and filtering this
ut. Input is basically anything you perceive through your senses—anything
can see, hear, smell, taste, or feel. It also includes your thoughts and your
gination, because the brain actually can't tell the difference between
t's real and what's imaginary, as confirmed in a study by Reddan et al.

This is fascinating because it means you can truly turn your dreams i reality!

So, maybe you're an introvert who just started a new leadership position. Y might be feeling nervous about attending your first directors-only meeti unsure of what to expect. You might have a thought like, *I don't know w I'm supposed to do . . . Do I talk? Or do I just watch?* That's when the brain g activated. It perceives your thought as a stress signal.

Because the thought serves as a stress signal, the sympathetic—or fight- flight—system gets activated. This leads to physical and mental experience stress, which are then sent to the body as output. You'll notice things l muscle tension, pain, nausea, poor digestion, anxiety, irritability, insom and so on. In this example, you might experience tight shoulders, swe palms, a tense stomach, queasiness, and more. Despite your best efforts to s alert and focused, you might be secretly panicking on the inside and not a to pay full attention.

I can't emphasize this enough: The mind-body connection is *powerful.* mind and body are not separate entities. They work together cohesively that you can function well.

So, now that you understand the stress pathway, there are three ways you take control and alter your stress response.

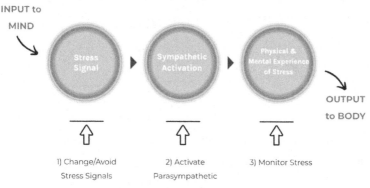

Figure 2.2: Mind-Body Connection/Stress Pathway Opportunities

As you see in Figure 2.2, you can:

1. Change and/or avoid stress signals to prevent the activation of the sympathetic system.
2. Activate your parasympathetic relaxation response to counter and switch off the fight-or-flight stress response.
3. Develop a way to monitor your stress so that you know what is going on. The quicker you become aware of it, the sooner you can respond by using one of the first two methods, and the easier it will be to reverse the effects of the stress response.

The other helpful thing to remember is that instead of activating the stress response, we can also actively cultivate a relaxation response that goes the other way instead.

Figure 2.3: Relaxation Response Pathway

As an example, imagine you are on vacation, relaxing on a quiet and beautiful beach. The weather is perfect, there's a gentle breeze, and the warm sun is shining down on you. You feel calm and relaxed.

If you look at Figure 2.3, you can see that the process starts with your brain filtering all the signals from your environment and interpreting them as a relaxation signal. This activates the parasympathetic response, which then gives you physical and mental experiences of relaxation. When the relaxation response is active, we feel calm and our muscles relax. We have a sense of peace in body and mind.

The goal is to recognize when you are activating the stress response and to actively reverse it into a relaxation response instead. Know that this is a process and gets easier the more you practice. It's a skill that you can get better at with practice, which is great news!

Throughout this book, you will learn various tools and approaches to help you master stress and regulate your fear response so you can have more of what you want with ease and become an inspiring success story.

Now, remember our goal as humans from an evolutionary perspective is to stay alive. Because of this, the brain has us focus on doing things to ensure our survival through the Motivational Triad.

The Motivational Triad has the brain focused on:

1. Seeking pleasure or comfort.
2. Avoiding pain or discomfort.
3. Conserving energy all the while, so that there's a good amount of energy saved up in case you end up needing it for some scary situation.

The perfect example of this pattern is when we procrastinate.

Let's say you've been wanting to start a side hustle because you're not feeling fulfilled in your day job. You have ideas about what you want to do and how to do it, but you just can't seem to get yourself to take the first step. Maybe that first step is talking to a lawyer or CPA about setting up the business entity or creating bylaws. But instead of doing those things, you procrastinate by checking your phone and scrolling through social media for hours, or going to eat a snack when you weren't even hungry. Does this resonate? I know I've done this when I have something I don't want to do.

So, let's break it down . . .

The reason you would rather scroll social media or eat cookies than sit down to find an attorney, especially if doing so is new to you, is because . . .

1. Social media and cookies are more familiar, safe, and comfortable, which fits into the "seek pleasure" part.
2. To do something new and different could be painful and dangerous, so procrastinating fits into the "avoid pain" part.
3. It takes work and brain power to sit down, do the research, and actually call somebody to help you set things up, but the brain doesn't want to use up excess energy, which fits into the "conserve energy" part.

I hope you now understand how procrastination is a perfect example of what the brain does, and that it's completely normal human behavior intended to ensure that we stay alive. Nothing has gone wrong. This happens to everyone.

So, what can we do about it? Now that you know how the brain defaults to this pattern, you can break the cycle so that you can get past it.

Before you get discouraged, thinking that it's "too hard" or "never going to work for me," I want you to know that it's possible to change.

Have you heard of the term *neuroplasticity*? It's the study of how the brain can adapt and change. Because new nerve cells are constantly being formed and connected, we can make new pathways in order to strengthen certain thoughts, beliefs, and habits that we like. This is akin to building toned arms by continuing to repeat bicep curls.

What's even more interesting is that in addition to building new connections, you can also take apart and weaken previous connections. It's like building Legos—you can put things together or take things apart. This is the best news ever! Because it means that you can let go of the past that isn't serving you and focus on what will be serving you instead.

In order to do so, you have to redirect the energy toward building new habits and pathways. Neural pathways are best strengthened when you are feeling relaxed because when you are under stress, the brain will default to the previous pathways rooted in survival instincts to keep you alive. This is why it's so important to learn how to manage your stress and regulate your nervous system.

So, now that you know that's possible, how do you go about doing it?

In order to change and do new things, your system has to believe that you are safe—otherwise it will sabotage you. Have you ever found yourself having

ther glass of wine at 9 p.m. when you said you weren't going to drink on
eekday? It's because there's a stronger power at play.

: key is to realize is that our brain is actually comprised of different parts.
n't worry, I'm not going to go into the nitty-gritty biochemical
1ponents, because I don't find them practical if you're not a biochemist or
archer looking at fMRI brain scans all day.

simplify, I want you to understand there are two parts to the brain: the
scious mind and the subconscious (unconscious) mind.

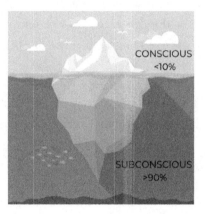

Figure 2.4: Conscious vs. Subconscious Mind Iceberg

: conscious mind contains the thoughts, feelings, memories, and desires
: we are aware of at any given moment. In contrast, the unconscious mind
ds the thoughts, feelings, memories, and desires that are *not* in our
scious awareness.

ording to cognitive neuroscientists and a study from Kihlstrom et al., we
y consciously use 5% of our cognitive capabilities. Meaning that *most* of
decisions, actions, emotions, and behaviors depend on this unconscious
o.

When I first learned this, I was a bit scared and confused. *What do you me*
I'm only using 5% of my capability? This is just the tip of the iceberg? How c
tap into this unconscious mind so that I can actually get what I want?

The problem is the unconscious mind is deeply rooted in our survi
mechanisms and instincts. And the human instinct to survive is our m
powerful drive. Whether we like it or not, our unconscious mind grea
controls our consciousness and our resultant behaviors.

You might be wondering why we are set up this way. Well, our brains c
only process a certain amount of input at a time. However, if we took c
sweet time to slowly sift through every piece of information, we proba
would be dead within a few seconds. Remember, our bodies are built for c
purpose: survival.

So, the brain evolved to rely on various fast-acting internal systems in order
quickly process information and respond. These fast-acting systems are bi
into the subconscious mind and able to override the conscious mind. Thi
why the subconscious mind is so powerful.

Now, fast forward millions of years: We live in a fast-paced world filled w
the latest tech gadgets and media. You may have heard the myth that c
attention span has shortened to that of a goldfish: a mere eight seconds.

Do you realize how many stimuli we have coming at us at every second? O
millions of "bits" or units of information. But our conscious mind can o
handle forty to fifty bits of information at a time—similar to our cavem
days. So, with this big gap, how do we manage?

There's a part of the brain called reticular activating system (RAS) that ser
as a filter for us. The RAS acts as a gatekeeper and is connected to all c
senses except smell. Its job is to quickly evaluate and prioritize all input, a

then instruct the brain on what to pay attention to and what it can safely ignore.

You can also think of the RAS like a search engine similar to Google. It can be used to look for positivity or negativity—whatever you type into the search bar. It only focuses on what you are thinking about (your search query), and it doesn't matter if those thoughts are positive or negative.

For example, if you're worried about not making enough money instead of focusing on the money you already have, the RAS will focus on filtering in all the evidence supporting the belief that you do *not* have enough money. You will be constantly reminded that you don't have enough and that things aren't working out. The RAS doesn't pay attention to all the good that's happening in your life. It will exaggerate everything that's *not* working and make you feel terrible.

On the other hand, if you are able to reprogram your beliefs and focus on all the money you already have, the RAS will focus on filtering in all the evidence supporting the belief that you lead an abundant life and have *more* than enough. You will be constantly reminded that everything is working out in your favor. The RAS will ignore any "bad" that's happening in your life. It will focus on everything that *is* working and make you feel great.

And remember that the brain prefers to be lazy and save energy based on the Motivational Triad. It likes to be comfortable. It wants to run on autopilot and keep things going as they are. If it ain't broke, don't fix it, right?

Now, autopilot does serve its purpose. If we had to use up energy to process every single thing all the time, the human species for sure wouldn't have survived. However, that still leaves us with a problem: What do we do when we're doing something that we *don't* like or that *isn't* serving us?

Therein lies the challenge. Because if we stay on autopilot and keep going down a rabbit hole to our worst nightmare, we will definitely not be happy when we finally arrive.

That's why it's so important to increase our awareness. To bring our subconscious patterns to the surface and expose them. Once we know what's going on, we have the power to change things for good.

When you know better, you do better.

Throughout this book, I will introduce you to different approaches to increasing awareness, most of which are built on a research-based foundation of mindfulness—which we will cover in depth in the next chapter.

QUESTIONS

1. What is an activity or action that puts me in a parasympathetic relaxation response?
2. What are my stress triggers? Where do I feel stress in the body?
3. How much of my day is spent on autopilot?

CHAPTER 3

BASICS OF MINDFULNESS

"I am not who you think I am. I am not who I think I am. I am who I think you think I am." —Charles Horton Cooley

What is mindfulness?

Mindfulness is the process of paying attention to the present moment on purpose, without judgment.

Let's break this down into three parts:

1. Paying attention: actively directing your focus
2. Present moment: remembering that life is happening right now, not in the past or the future
3. Without judgment: observing and experiencing the reality without determining if it's "good" or "bad"

Mindfulness is not just about paying attention. It's about *how* we pay attention.

In order to better understand, I will review the basic principles of mindfulness here.

Warning: These may sound simple, but it doesn't mean they're easy.

I like to start with one of the most fundamental concepts: **non-judgment**. This was one of the hardest things for me to learn and practice.

We're human. We judge. That's what we do! We like to say this is right, that is wrong. This is good, that is bad. We have been conditioned to look for certainty and use black-and-white thinking.

As I started to study the practice of mindfulness, I realized how often I was viewing the world through a lens of judgment. Toward everything, everyone else, and especially myself.

I judged others when their beliefs and values weren't congruent with my own, and focused on division instead of inclusion. I judged myself when I made a mistake, when I didn't get the result I was hoping for. I thought I had to be hard on myself because if not, *who's going to keep me accountable? How can I make sure to achieve and succeed?*

But in reality, judgments are a filter and veil that keep us from seeing things as they really are.

As I mentioned in the last chapter, our brain is very good at filtering information. It only shows us what we want to see. So even though we are all living in the same time and world, every person actually has a different experience depending on their own brain patterns and filters.

It's like trying to maintain eye contact with a person on the first date as they're about to share something personal, but your glasses keep fogging up with steam from the hot soup you ordered. (Which, by the way, note to self: That was awkward. Maybe order something else next time?)

So how do you wipe those glasses clean?

By developing a practice of non-judgment. Which is much easier said than done, I know. But it's possible. Non-judgment is about being willing to see

ıgs as they actually are in the present moment. A way to be open and okay
h what is.

n-judgment allows us to be authentic in how we view and respond, because
are responding to the actual thing, not our perception of the thing.

an exercise, I like to repeat and remind myself: *I am not my thoughts. I am
ɔly the observer.* This allows me to take a more removed stance and be an
ective third party—toward the world and my own thoughts—as best as I

so ask myself how it feels in my body when I am in a state of judgment
sus non-judgment. Do the following exercise with me.

XERCISE: FEELINGS AS SENSATIONS IN THE BODY

Think about a time when you felt judged and also judged in
response . . .

Maybe it was by that nosy third aunt at a family gathering when
she snarkily asked, "You're still single?" or "When are you going to get
a *real* job?"

What are your initial thoughts and responses to this memory?
And how did it make you feel when it first happened? Close your eyes
and take yourself back to that moment in time.

You might have thoughts like, *Ugh, this is why I hate our large
family gatherings. I should have gotten another drink first. She's the worst.*
You might respond with a polite smile even though you secretly want
to yell at her to leave you alone.

As you think about the incident, what sensations do you feel in your body? Tightness? Heaviness? Numbness? Tingling? Pay attention to where any feelings are located.

Now, take a few deep breaths to reset. Feel your feet on the ground. Remind yourself that you are safe in this moment.

Once you've centered yourself, think back to the same moment in time and let yourself hear the same exact words. But this time, use a lens of non-judgment instead—meaning not jumping to conclusions and reacting, but rather thinking about how an objective third party would respond.

For example, can you agree that your relative is simply speaking words out of her mouth? Words that may or may not make sense, and that you might respond to in different ways, depending how you interpret them?

When you are able to diffuse and neutralize, you are in a state of non-judgment.

HINT: Nothing is good or bad. It just is.

The moment we label something as good or bad, right or wrong, that is when judgment creeps in. It's sneaky like that!

So, a big part of practicing mindfulness is learning to adopt a sense of non-judgment and become an impartial witness.

The next part is to maintain a sense of **curiosity** and retain a **beginner's mind**. The easiest way to do that is to think back to what it's like when you're learning something new—when you're a beginner. It doesn't matter how old you are; there's a sense of wonder and awe because everything is new to you.

It's like visiting a new country for the first time or learning a new language. You can be curious because there's infinite possibility.

By the way, do you ever get frustrated when you're learning something new? Like, maybe you feel like you should have remembered it by now, or it should be much easier, or you should be further along. I want you to recognize that this is judgment talking. See how tricky it is? Anytime you hear or say the word *should*, I want you to pause and notice it. Say to yourself, *This is judgment. I choose to release it.*

In addition to having a beginner's mind, it's important to practice **acceptance** of what is. I always like to emphasize that acceptance does *not* mean condoning something. Rather, it's an acknowledgement of what's actually going on.

A lot of times, we suffer because we're unhappy with how things are and we don't want to let that unhappiness go. As a result, we'll try to force things to go our way, which often leads to more stress down the line.

Instead, I invite you to consider acceptance as the *first* step, the one that lets you start to see and acknowledge that things are not what you imagined. Remember that we can't change what we don't know. If you don't know something, how do you know you need to change it, right? It all starts with awareness.

Once you experience acceptance, it's helpful to be in a state of **non-striving**. This doesn't mean that you do nothing and lie there like a dead fish. On the contrary, it means being fully present in the moment without having to change it. Allow yourself to notice all the thoughts and feel the sensations that are coming up for you.

A good practice is to pay attention to your five senses. We are always receiving input from our external environment (over millions of bits, remember?). We also experience sensations in our physical body. Whether that's tingling, tightness, warmth, heaviness, coolness, you name it. All of that is feeding into our brain as input, which our brain is actively processing to assess if we are in a dangerous situation or not. To see if we need to activate the fight-or-flight sympathetic system, or if it's safe to relax.

Let's see how aware you are. Do this fun exercise with me.

EXERCISE: FIVE SENSES EXPERIENCE

Take a breath. Notice . . .

Five things you see.
Four things you feel.
Three things you hear.
Two things you smell.
One thing you taste.

Did you do it? How was the experience for you? What did you notice that you didn't before?

I wonder if you experienced any sensations in your body. How did it feel?

Did you know that feelings are simply sensations in the body?

When we have "positive" and "negative" feelings, our body responds accordingly. We've been trained to avoid and resist so-called "negative" feelings because they're uncomfortable. Negative feelings such as shame, guilt, embarrassment, anger, pain, sadness, and so on. Remember, the brain seeks comfort and the familiar because that's what's "safe."

But I want you to start seeing feelings as simply sensations in the body. Those sensations are the language of the body—how the body communicates with us.

When you recognize your feelings as sensations, remain in a state of non-judgment and non-striving and describe the sensations in order to process them. So-called "negative" feelings will actually pass through you much quicker than they would otherwise, and you will feel better soon after.

I work with a lot of high achievers who want to have more in life and be unstoppable. Do you want to know the number-one secret I share with them?

It's to learn how to feel your feelings. Feel the sensations without avoidance, distraction, or resistance. No pushing them away with overeating, overdrinking, bingeing shows, over-scrolling. None of that.

Imagine if you were open to feeling fear, anxiety, rejection, shame, embarrassment, pain, sadness, guilt, anger, anything! What would that life look like?

As a recovering perfectionist, I used to be terrified of making mistakes and failing. I was also really worried about being judged. And then I realized how much those fears were holding me back.

So I learned this very important skill, to feel your feelings, and am so grateful I get to share this with you so that *you* can be successful and live your best life.

Note: I know for some people it can be hard to "feel" things. If this is you, I want to reassure you that you are fully capable of experiencing sensations. However, there may have been some experiences in your past (often traumatic in nature) that caused your system to turn down the volume as a protective mechanism, so that you are not able to perceive sensations as well. But if you are willing to stay open and aware, you can retrain your system and will be able to turn the dial up and hear the music again. I also recommend working with specialized somatic therapists to help yourself heal and regain awareness.

Now, it is crucial to mention **patience**. I know we often want things to work out perfectly, like, yesterday. But things unfold in their own way. This is not a race. We are all here on our own journeys, with our own lessons to learn. In today's comparison culture, it can be challenging to stay in your own lane. But we cannot compare our beginnings to someone else's ending.

One of the most interesting practices is to pay attention to when you are feeling envious of what others have. Pause and ask yourself, "So what?" Envy reveals so much more about how you feel about yourself than the other person.

And notice when you are in a rush to get somewhere or something done. If you're rushing, it means you aren't present. We like to think we have control over things, but the reality is, we can only control ourselves.

Along with that, we have to build **trust** in ourselves and each other. Know that all we have is the present moment. Trust that things are working out for the greatest good of all. Again, easier said than done, I know.

One thing I like to remind myself is that I will get either the results I want or the lessons I need. This helps me stay open and receptive to all the learning opportunities out there, as I truly believe we are all here to grow and evolve into the best versions of ourselves.

And remember, there is so much power in **letting go**. Allowing things to be as they are. When we are grasping and clinging on for dear life, it means we are not fully trusting. We do not trust that what we yearn for is ours. We do not trust that we are capable or enough. It means we are caught up in the desire to control what we don't have control over.

Lastly, I always like to end with **gratitude** and **generosity**. When we are in a state of gratitude, we are cultivating a state of abundance. We believe that we are enough, right now, in this moment. We are content. We are calm. We are at peace. When we believe we are in a state of sufficiency and enough-ness, we are naturally more generous and forgiving with ourselves and others.

SO MUCH BETTER

titude is also one of the best ways for us to deepen our connections with another. Being thankful for every experience and interaction. Because n if it is unpleasant, it is an opportunity to confirm what you like and ike and to get to know yourself even better.

I hope you are understanding that mindfulness is a process and way of life. an approach to observation.

en you have full awareness of what's going on, you have the freedom and ver to choose what to do next. And in doing so, you can relieve your "ering.

a won't continue to spend all day wasting your energy solving for X when real problem is actually Y.

d how do you *actually* practice mindfulness, on a practical level? You will various tools and practices throughout the book, but I want you to tember the goal of mindfulness is to be fully present and to fully be urself.

learning to move from constantly "doing" into "being." We are human ngs, not human doings, right?

ile many people may equate mindfulness with monks and meditation, ase know that you can be mindful while doing anything. You don't need sign up for a ten-day silent retreat and go sit atop a mountain to be indful." You can be mindful right now—sitting, reading, breathing, eating, king, even showering or doing the dishes.

netimes, people want to practice mindfulness because they think it will ke their thoughts go away. Unfortunately, that's not how it works.

ndfulness is the practice of becoming more aware and accepting of *all* parts he experience, including thinking. It's not about suppressing thoughts or

- 41 -

anything else. Controlling your thoughts or being without thoughts is *not* goal of mindfulness.

Plus, why would you want to be without thoughts? Your thoughts are w fuel you (if you learn how to use them properly, that is; more on this Chapter 7).

And remember, there is no perfect way to practice mindfulness. It's not ab sitting and meditating for hours every day. It's about learning new ways sense, understand, and respond to your life.

Every little bit counts.

Wherever you are now is exactly where you need to be.

Please be kind to yourself.

Mindfulness is not about getting to a destination, because *there* is not be than *here*. The problems you have now will still be there later if you are paying attention. They might even be magnified because they have continu to grow without you tending to them.

Learn to be open to what is, so that you don't struggle when you arrive.

Look at the picture in Figure 3.1 and ask yourself, which one are you?

Mind Full, or Mindful?

Figure 3.1: Mind Full vs. Mindful

RECAP: Principles of Mindfulness

1. Non-judgment
2. Curiosity/beginner's mind
3. Acceptance
4. Non-striving
5. Patience
6. Trust
7. Letting go/letting be
8. Gratitude
9. Generosity

QUESTIONS

1. Which of these principles is easy for me? Why?
2. Which of these principles is hard for me? Why?
3. How can I incorporate these principles into my daily life?

PART II

SELF-ASSESSMENT

Are you ready to be an example of what's possible?

This is your one precious life. Design it how you want.

Stop wasting time.

Let's see where things are at and how to change it for good. Learn about the Inspiring Success Story Method™ and the three fundamental pillars to go beyond your comfort zone, transcend adversity, and manifest your true potential with ease.

CHAPTER 4

WHERE ARE YOU

"Every expert was once a beginner." —Helen Hayes

at if there's a way for you to get what you want in life?

at if you're not supposed to be struggling? What if it could be easy?

NT: **What if your success was inevitable?**

ant you to know that you are here because you have important gifts to e. Some of which may not have been uncovered yet.

ough working with many clients, I have found the greatest joy in helping ple go from unfulfilled high achievers to inspiring success stories.

re is something magical about being able to express yourself authentically be appreciated for who you really are.

ive identified three pillars of mastery in order to make this successful sition with ease, based on my years of experience. The rest of the book is ded into each of the pillars so that you can easily reference them.

ve a quick assessment for you to determine which pillar(s) to prioritize, as as the tier you may fall under depending on your results and what to do t.

Want the results emailed to you? Take the quiz by scanning the QR code below:

cindytsaimd.com/quiz

EXERCISE: ASSESSMENT

Read each statement and select the option that best describes how often you experience the statement. Don't overthink it. No one is watching. Pick the first option that comes to mind.

Question	Statement	Rarely/on occasion	Some of the time	Most of the time	Almost always
1	I know how to stay calm, even in new, unfamiliar, or high-pressure situations.	1	2	3	4
2	I can sit with uncomfortable feelings without getting distracted by my phone, food, alcohol, TV, etc.	1	2	3	4
3	I know how to work with and manage my inner critic.	1	2	3	4
4	I believe I am enough and am here to do great things.	1	2	3	4
5	I make it a priority to reflect frequently so I can head in the best direction for myself.	1	2	3	4
6	I see myself as a creative person.	1	2	3	4
	SUM OF EACH COLUMN				
	TOTAL				

RESULTS: (Reference Figure 4.1 below and further explanations for details.)

If your score is 14 or less, you are likely an "unfulfilled high achiever."

If your score is between 15 and 18, you are likely a "rule-abiding expert."

If your score is between 19 and 23, you are likely a "reserved problem solver."

If your score is 24, congratulations! You are an "inspiring success story."

Reach out to me (**hello@cindytsaimd.com**) to see how we can collaborate and help others be the best they can be!

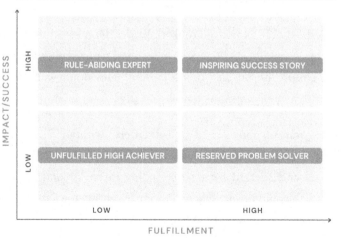

Figure 4.1: Inspiring Success Story Method^{TM} Matrix

Each tier occupies a different area of the matrix depending on the level of impact/success and fulfillment.

<u>UNFULFILLED HIGH ACHIEVER</u>

SYMPTOMS: You've been doing all the right things and checking all the boxes. You get exhausted easily and worry about burning out. You may have poor boundaries and challenges with work-life balance. You experience self-doubt and self-criticism frequently, often comparing yourself to others, wishing things looked different. But you tell yourself you have a "good" life and you think you *should* be happy when you're not. You feel like there's something missing, but you're not sure what to do next and can't quite put your finger on it. Or you simply have no time because you've already overcommitted for the next three weeks.

CAUSES: The high achiever has lost connection with who they really are. Chronic stress has triggered the system (mind and body) to remain in a state of high alert and survival mode which prevents access to their true potential. They have been conditioned to focus on external validation and comparison culture.

BELIEFS & EMOTIONS: Need to work harder. Don't stop. Keep going. It will get better when _____. Stuck in fear and worried about what others will think. Unsure if you are "doing it right" and don't want to make a mistake.

JOURNEY: Starting process of self-discovery without clear direction. Experiencing emotional roller coaster or feeling complacent at times. Overwhelmed and stressed by a never-ending to-do list and see countless resources available, but unsure where to begin. Wanting to change but having hard time being consistent and following through.

RULE-ABIDING EXPERT

SYMPTOMS: You've experienced high levels of success and are respected as an expert in your field. Everything looks good, except for one *tiny* problem. You don't feel fulfilled. You're great at following the rules, but you often feel like a cog in the wheel and similar to many of your colleagues. You get nervous when you're asked to do things outside your normal activities, worried if it will detract from your status. You're so focused on doing the work right that you often forget to bring in the fun and play.

CAUSES: The rule-abiding expert maintains some connection with the self but prefers to stay in their comfort zone. The desire to avoid chaos and conflict is more important than deep personal fulfillment.

BELIEFS & EMOTIONS: You feel good because you're successful but sometimes feel unsure if this is what you're meant to do. You are confident most of the time but know there is more you could do if you really wanted to. But things are fine, so not going to think about it.

JOURNEY: There is a level of self-awareness but a resistance to fully grow and evolve—to become fully fulfilled. Stress is still an ongoing issue but are open to exploring ways around this. There is some bandwidth to invest in self but unsure if ready to fully commit for good.

RESERVED PROBLEM SOLVER

SYMPTOMS: You are curious and know you hold the answers to many problems. But you prefer to keep your thoughts and ideas to yourself and your inner circle. You are self-aware and speak up only when it really matters or when someone asks for your opinion. You wish you had more confidence to put things out there. You like to take your time before acting on your thoughts, but sometimes miss opportunities to share and make a bigger impact.

CAUSES: The reserved problem solver prefers to stay out of the limelight because it can be uncomfortable to be seen. There is a level of independence and autonomy that it is important to them to maintain.

BELIEFS & EMOTIONS: You are comfortable and likely happy in your bubble. You know that you could help more people but may still believe that it's "too hard to convince people" so decide against changing anything and sharing your gifts with the world.

JOURNEY: They have a good sense of who they are and enjoy most days. Though the inner critic and imposter syndrome can creep in sometimes which makes them want to retreat even further. There is a grounded curiosity to explore how life could be better.

INSPIRING SUCCESS STORY

SYMPTOMS: You have done a lot of work and healing on yourself. You are calm and secure in who you really are. You are confident and creative in your endeavors. You are making a great impact in your own way and feeling good about it.

CAUSES: The inspiring success story has leaned into who they are, shut off the external noise, and understood that true validation comes from within. They have committed to investing in their own growth and are able to think critically and for themselves. They have learned how to work with their inner critic and embraced fear while taking empowering actions to further their success.

BELIEFS & EMOTIONS: You know that you are enough, just as you are, right now. Deeply humbled by your accomplishments and everything the world has to offer. Knowing that you have a lot to offer and gifts that only you can share. Here to inspire and be of service. Grateful and living with a strong sense of abundance.

URNEY: You know that life is a journey and that anything is possible. As
felong learner, you seek out new challenges and have fun while being the
t you can be.

* * *

w, how do you become an inspiring success story?

er working with many clients and reflecting on my own journey, I noticed
t there were some recurrent themes. This led me to developing my unique
cess: the Inspiring Success Story Method™.

e key is through mastering the three pillars: **calm**, **confidence**, and
iosity! Refer to Figure 4.2 for details.

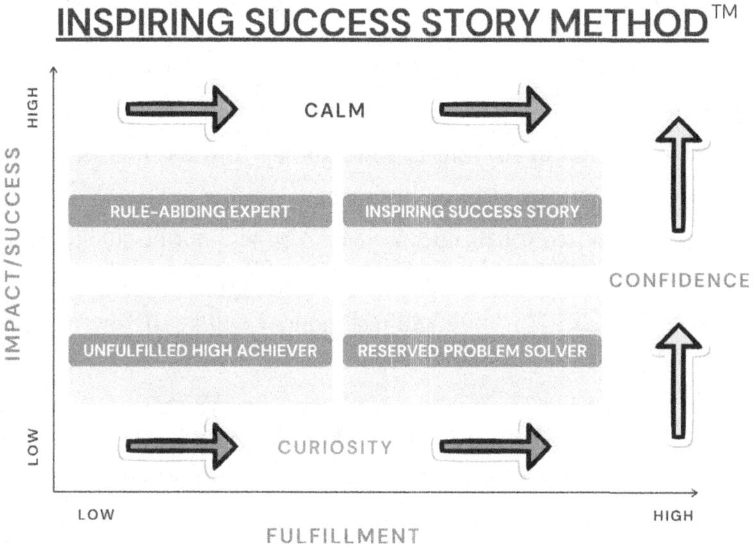

INSPIRING SUCCESS STORY METHOD™

Figure 4.2: Inspiring Success Story Method™ Mastery

ese three fundamental pillars exist in each tier at differing levels. Read on
understand the breakdown of each pillar and why it's crucial to have all
ee working together in harmony.

Figure 4.3: The Three Pillars of the Inspiring Success Story Method^{TM}

The "calm" pillar focuses on regulating your nervous system so that you be grounded and secure. You already know our brains are wired for surviv and constantly scanning for threats. Modern-day "threats" may be request a raise or going on a first date with someone you met online. When the response gets activated (often unconscious), you will not be able to relax a be your true self. Hence, it's crucial to develop your own internal sense safety through the various tools and techniques I will be sharing with you Part III of this book.

The "confidence" pillar focuses on developing a strong sense of self-bel This is when you unlearn old programming and rewire the brain. You exam and let go of old thought patterns and beliefs, and actively create new o that will catapult you to success. As shown by the research in neuroplastic the brain's nerve cells can make new pathways to strengthen thoughts, beli and habits that we like. This is akin to building toned arms by repeating bi curls. You will learn some of my best tricks in Part IV.

The "curiosity" pillar focuses on finding creativity, fun, and connecting w your true self and wisdom. We all have our own gifts to share, but when y are disconnected, it's like walking in a maze, blindfolded. You're already lost, and on top of that, you can't see. I am excited to share some practical tips and great activities with you in Part V.

There is a reason all three components are necessary to become an inspiring success story.

COMBINATION	RESULT	MISSING
CALM + CONFIDENCE	• Can handle high-pressure situations. • Believe in yourself. • *But,* are so focused on *doing* that you lose sight of the bigger picture, don't have fun, or run out of ideas and lose your connection to the self.	CURIOSITY
CONFIDENCE + CURIOSITY	• Believe in yourself. • Have fun and are connected with who you are. • *But,* can get stuck because you don't feel grounded and secure, so the subconscious takes over. You take five steps forward, four steps back, and net only one step forward.	CALM
CURIOSITY + CALM	• Have fun and are connected with who you are. • Can handle high-pressure situations. • *But,* are still using old programming and beliefs and don't take calculated risks that bring you to success and fulfillment.	CONFIDENCE

Now that you understand the framework, let's dive into each of the pillars!

I have included links to various videos, recordings, and resources throughout this book to support you on your journey. But know that you don't have to do this alone.

At any point, please email me (hello@cindytsaimd.com) and let me know how it's going!

I look forward to hearing from you. :)

QUESTIONS

1. Which pillar is my strength?
2. Which pillar is my greatest area of opportunity?
3. Am I ready to get out of my comfort zone and take my life to the next level?

PART III

CALM

Change happens at the speed of safety.

After years practicing as a primary care physician, I found that inflammation is at the core of many diseases. Mastering the pillar of calm and regulating your nervous system is one of the best ways to decrease inflammation and stress. In this section, I'll walk you through some of the easiest methods that can jump-start your journey.

This book is not meant to provide medical advice and will not be offering specific lifestyle recommendations, though I recognize that those can be very important in developing calm. I truly believe you deserve your own personalized approach to achieve the best results and encourage you to work with a practitioner who is able to see the whole picture.

Listen to and take care of your body, because you only get one!

CHAPTER 5

BREATHING

"You breathe oxygen? We have so much in common."
—Unknown

r breath is powerful.

athing is something we do all day but seldom give much thought to. It's of those things we take for granted. But when used effectively, it can bring mmense calm.

athing allows us to bring fresh oxygen into our body. Oxygen is what rishes our cells and fuels the metabolic processes that keep us alive.

athing allows us to remove carbon dioxide from our body. All the toxic te products that aren't serving us anymore.

there are different breathing techniques that can make this process more ctive. Our breath becomes powerful the moment we choose to focus on it.

nentioned in Chapter 2, our brain is focused on keeping us alive. It uses internal messenger system called the autonomic nervous system to imunicate with all the different organ systems and make sure they are ctioning properly.

When we are in a state of stress or panic, our brain activates the sympathe[tic] nervous system, which makes our organs work extra hard in order to prot[ect] us from harm. However, these days, most of the threats we face are not actua[lly] life-threatening—for instance, your chances of being eaten by a lion [are] thankfully very low! Unless you're on an African safari (in which case, ple[ase] be careful and follow your guide's recommendations).

So, the question becomes, how can we deactivate the stress response a[nd] prompt relaxation instead? Well, deep breathing is one of the most effect[ive] ways to activate the parasympathetic nervous system—the one that is in cha[rge] of helping you relax.

Breathing retrains our nervous system response and allows us to pause inst[ead] of jumping and reacting. There have been studies, including one from Zacc[aro] et al., showing that the benefits of regular deep breathing include:

- Improved mood
- Stronger immune system
- Increased energy
- Improved digestion
- And much more . . .

You may remember my discussion of the vagus nerve, which is the [main] conductor/controller of the parasympathetic nervous system. It comes out [of] the brain, down the side of the neck, and into the chest and abdominal cavi[ty].

You might think you don't have any control over this random nerve in [the] middle of your chest. But you actually do! Every time you take a deep brea[th] your lungs expand fully. When the lungs are fully expanded, they rub [up] against the vagus nerve to stimulate and activate it! It's the easiest trick [to] increase vagal tone!

As the vagus nerve gets activated, it sends signals to your brain to prom[pt] relaxation. All your organs start to slow down (in a good way) and a sense calm overtakes you. And yes, there are many other ways to activate the vagus nerve, many of which I teach in my programs, but here we will focus specifically on different breathing techniques to help promote relaxation, in order to keep it simple.

Now, taking breaths is also one of the easiest ways to practice mindfulness. Remember that mindfulness is all about being present in the current moment without judgment. When you put your focus on your breath, every inhale and exhale, you are bringing awareness to your body and the present moment.

So, how do you do this?

Before we start, I want you to know that this does not need to take a long time. Breathing exercises are quick, requiring only a few seconds out of your day for you to reap the benefits. Plan time throughout your day to take a break and breathe deeply. I like to set a few recurring breathing alarms on my phone every day to prompt myself to pause and take some breaths.

I also want you to know that you can practice anytime, anywhere. It's simple and you don't need any special tools or equipment. Anytime you feel like it, you can do it! How great is that!

There are so many different breathing techniques, it can get overwhelming and feel like a Vegas buffet sometimes. As I like to say, everyone is different, and the things you need will be different. I have shared some of my favorite techniques here that work well for my clients. Certain techniques will appeal to you and not to others, and that's completely fine.

HINT: Remember—you are here on your journey.

And please know that it's normal for thoughts to come up in the process.

Some people think that they're doing it "wrong" when they can't focus on their breath because they have a busy mind. It may be challenging in the beginning, but it gets easier the more you do it. I recommend you view your thoughts as clouds in the sky, simply drifting by, going about the day. Anytime you notice you're getting distracted thinking about something else, consciously redirect and bring your focus back to your breath.

I have included videos to each of the techniques, so make sure to scan the QR code and watch the guided demonstrations! For each of these techniques, I encourage you to set a timer for two minutes (or your preferred length of time) and practice each one to see how it feels for you.

Whether you like or don't like the technique, pause and ask yourself *why*. Be open to what is. The most important thing is to find what works for *you*.

To start, find a comfortable position. I generally recommend being seated instead of lying down because sometimes people get too comfortable and they immediately fall asleep! (Which is fine too, but might be a sign that you're not getting enough quality sleep at night . . . A conversation for another day!)

Also, turn off your notifications. This is your time. You deserve it!

If you are seated, keep both your feet flat on the ground and feel your back and butt supported by the seat beneath you. You may also try doing this sitting cross-legged on a yoga mat. Sit upright yet relaxed. Allow your shoulders to drop and arms to rest gently beside you or on your lap. Close your eyes or maintain a soft, downward gaze in front of you. Now, let's begin.

cindytsaimd.com/somuchbetterbookgift

TECHNIQUE #1: CLEANSING BREATH

1. Check in with yourself: on a scale of 1–10 (10 being the best you've ever felt), how do you feel now?

2. Inhale through the nose and exhale through an open-mouthed "ahhh."

    With each inhale, allow the chest to expand fully and feel oxygen entering the body to nourish all your cells.

    With each exhale, allow the chest to release all the air and stress that is hanging over you and keeping you stuck. With each inhale, feel cleansed and energized. With each exhale, feel lighter and calmer. Continue to take a few breaths at your own pace.

3. Check in with yourself: On a scale of 1–10 (10 being the best you've ever felt), how do you feel after? How easy was this technique for you?

TECHNIQUE #2: 4-6 BREATHING

1. Check in with yourself: On a scale of 1–10 (10 being the best you've ever felt), how do you feel now?

2. Inhale through the nose for a count of 4, then slowly exhale through the mouth for a count of 6.

    With each 4-count inhale, feel the chest expand. You can focus on the counting and take a full, deep breath to expand the lungs and activate the vagus nerve for parasympathetic relaxation.

    With each 6-count exhale, slowly allowing the air to leave your body. Repeat for a few rounds at your own pace.

1. Check in with yourself: On a scale of 1–10 (10 being the best you've ever felt), how do you feel after? How easy was this technique for you?

ECHNIQUE #3: 4-7-8 BREATHING

1. Check in with yourself: On a scale of 1–10 (10 being the best you've ever felt), how do you feel now?

2. Inhale through the nose for a count of 4, hold your breath for a count of 7, and then exhale completely through the mouth for a count of 8. Repeat a few rounds at your own pace.

   This is one of most helpful techniques to reduce anxiety and help people get to sleep, in part because this controlled breathing method forces the mind and body to focus on the breath rather than replay endless worries and stresses.

3. Check in with yourself: On a scale of 1–10 (10 being the best you've ever felt), how do you feel after? How easy was this technique for you?

TECHNIQUE #4: BOX BREATHING

1. Check in with yourself: On a scale of 1–10 (10 being the be you've ever felt), how do you feel now?

2. Picture a box or square in your mind with four equal-length side You will inhale, hold your breath, exhale, and hold your breath– each for a count of 4. Ready?

   Breathe in, counting to 4 slowly, feeling the air enter your lungs

   Hold your breath for 4 counts.

   Slowly exhale through your mouth for 4 counts.

   Hold your breath for 4 counts. Repeat a few times at your ow pace.

   This is one of the techniques Navy SEALS train in to redu stress.

3. Check in with yourself: On a scale of 1–10 (10 being the be you've ever felt), how do you feel after? How easy was th technique for you?

TECHNIQUE #5: DEEP BELLY/DIAPHRAGMATIC BREATHING

1. Check in with yourself: On a scale of 1–10 (10 being the best you've ever felt), how do you feel now?

2. Put one hand on your belly just below the ribs and the other hand on your chest.

   Take a deep breath in through the nose, letting the air in deeply, toward the lower belly. The hand on your chest should remain still, while the one on your belly should be pushed out.

   Now contract your abdominal muscles and let the belly come inward as you exhale through pursed lips. The hand on the belly should move back to its original position.

   Repeat for a few rounds at your own pace.

   This technique helps to strengthen the diaphragm, one of the most important breathing muscles, which helps ensure we get full oxygen exchange. There are also vagus nerve endings by the abdomen, making this a great way to slow your heartbeat and lower blood pressure.

3. Check in with yourself: On a scale of 1–10 (10 being the best you've ever felt), how do you feel after? How easy was this technique for you?

Okay, so I hope you gave these breathing techniques a try and found at least one or two that are easy for you to incorporate into your day. It's recommended that you practice intentional breathing at least two to three times a day. Find ways to fit it into your schedule. Pay attention to how you feel before and after breathing.

Know that it doesn't take long. You can do it!

QUESTIONS

1. How often do I pay attention to my breath?
2. Which breathing technique did I enjoy most?
3. How and when can I incorporate intentional breaths into my day?

CHAPTER 6

EMOTIONAL FREEDOM TECHNIQUE (EFT)

"I'm afraid of needles, except acupuncture needles."
—*Catherine O'Hara*

Are you afraid of needles?

You're not alone. I always look away when I get my blood drawn. (And make sure I drink a ton of water beforehand so they don't have issues finding veins, because being poked once is bad enough, let alone three times.)

When I first learned about acupuncture, I was hesitant to try it because I didn't want to be poked and have needles sticking out of me like a porcupine. But I learned how it was an ancient healing practice that was very effective in recreating balance and calm in the body. So, of course, I knew I had to try.

Though for people who prefer not to get poked and don't want to go visit an acupuncturist, I have good news for you.

Introducing . . . Emotional Freedom Technique, or EFT (a.k.a. "tapping").

Did you know that by tapping on various points on the body, you can balance energy and reduce emotional and physical pain? You can regulate the nervous system and create your own calm! Even though we can't "see" energy, it is very much related to our physical body.

EFT is a method developed by engineer Gary Craig in the 1990s. It is based on the principle in Traditional Chinese Medicine that our body contains an invisible network of energy pathways called meridians.

Imagine the meridians as channels or highways that run through every human body and are connected to various organ systems. There are twelve major meridians with over four hundred acupuncture points.

These acupuncture points resemble the various exits on a highway where cars can merge on or off. They identify areas of more concentrated energy, and also potential areas of blockage or traffic. Acupuncture needles are inserted into specific acupuncture points to release any blockages so that energy can flow smoothly.

In EFT, instead of inserting needles, you use your fingers to tap on specific points to apply pressure while bringing attention to specific thoughts and feelings you wish to resolve. EFT allows you to release and transform uncomfortable feelings and sensations that are impacting your experience. After a few rounds of tapping, people often report feeling lighter, calmer, and generally better overall. It's quite amazing, really.

You might be skeptical about how this works. Remember that the mind and body are intricately connected. Because thoughts are the language of the mind and feelings are the language of the body, EFT offers a way to work with both the mind and body to shift your thoughts, feelings, and physical responses (e.g. stress or tension).

Even if you are new to identifying specific emotions, you usually can tell if you're feeling "bad" and "low energy" or feeling "good" and "high energy."

So often, we get stuck in old patterns and beliefs, and it's hard to pull ourselves out from the hole we have dug for ourselves. When we are feeling stressed, it's

ally because we are in "survival mode" and the primitive part of our brain
u may have heard of the term *amygdala*) has taken over.

at's when the fight-or-flight response is activated, and the body releases
ious chemicals like the stress hormones cortisol and adrenaline, which
rease the stress response. When this chain of reactions is activated, words
ne cannot reach the parts of the brain needed to calm us down. This is
ause words are connected to the rational language centers located in a
erent part of the brain (the prefrontal cortex), not these primitive areas.

through tapping and stimulation of various acupressure points, you can
onnect to the primitive areas and calm the amygdala, facilitating the release
alming chemicals instead. This brings you to a more relaxed and grounded
e. As cortisol levels decrease, your body will be able to regulate and get
k into balance again. This is one of the best ways to create your own safety
our system.

here's the process. Scan the QR code to watch my tutorial video! I have
luded a detailed step-by-step guide below.

cindytsaimd.com/somuchbetterbookgift

1. Have a sip of water. It's important to be hydrated during this process.
2. Identify something that is bothering you. This issue can be a feeling
   in your body or a thought in your mind. Let's name the issue "stress."

3. Rate the intensity of this issue on a scale of 0–10 (where 10 is th
   worst, 0 is nonexistent). How intense is this particular "stress"?

4. Prepare a phrase to repeat using the format: "Even though I have thi
   'stress' (replace with whatever issue you have), I deeply and completel
   accept myself."

5. Identify the various tapping points (nine total), as shown below i
   Figure 6.1.

Start tapping on these points in order, stating the phrases an
repeating the rounds below as guided. Use 2 or 3 fingers to tap. (
prefer my index and middle fingers, but do what feels comfortable t
you.)

The tapping pressure should be firm with a slight bounce, but no
forceful. More force does not equate more benefit. The goal is to fee
the pressure but not be in pain. You can tap one side or both sides o
the face/body. It is normal to experience some sensations in your bod
during tapping. Use this as a mindfulness practice to simply observ
what you're feeling.

Tapping Points

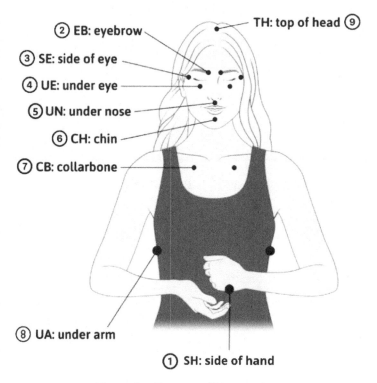

Figure 6.1: Location of Tapping Points

1. Side of Hand (SH): located on either hand on the outside fleshy part that you would use to karate chop something.
2. Eyebrow Point (EB): where the eyebrows begin, close to the bridge of the nose.
3. Side of Eye (SE): on the bone directly along the outside of either eye.
4. Under Eye (UE): on the bone directly underneath either eye.
5. Under Nose (UN): the area beneath the nose and above the upper lip.
6. Chin Point (CH): the area below your bottom lip and above the chin, right in the crease.

7. Collarbone Point (CB): starting from where your collar bones meet in the center, go down an inch and out an inch on either side.
8. Under Arm (UA): on the side of body, about four inches beneath the armpit.
9. Top of Head (TH): located directly in the center of the top of the head.

Check in and reassess your intensity rating. Has the number changed? If your number is greater than 0, repeat the tapping process again.

EXERCISE: DETAILED TAPPING PROCESS FOR STRESS

Scan QR code to watch my tutorial video!

-   Take a sip of water.
-   Take some deep breaths.
-   Notice your "stress." How intense is this stress? Rate the intensity on a scale of 0–10.

Round 1:

-   Tapping on the side of hand (SH) point, repeat the following phrase three times: "Even though I have this stress, I deeply and completely accept myself."
-   Tap the eyebrow point (EB) 7–10 times while repeating the phrase: "This stress . . ."
-   Tap the side of eye point (SE) 7–10 times while repeating the phrase: "So much stress . . ."
-   Tap the under eye point (UE) 7–10 times while repeating the phrase: "This stress . . . I feel it in my _____" (describe where you are feeling the stress, e.g. my chest, my shoulders, my neck . . .).

- Tap the under nose point (UN) 7–10 times while repeating the phrase: "So stressed . . . More than my body can handle . . ."
- Tap the chin point (CH) 7–10 times while repeating the phrase: "It's exhausting . . . so overwhelming . . ."
- Tap the collarbone point (CB) 7–10 times while repeating the phrase: "All this stress . . ."
- Tap the under arm point (UA) 7–10 times while repeating the phrase: "So stressed . . ."
- Tap the top of head point (TH) 7–10 times while repeating the phrase: "All this stress . . ."

Round 2:

- Tap the eyebrow point (EB) 7–10 times while repeating the phrase: "Even though I'm still stressed, I'm willing to love and accept myself anyway."
- Tap the side of eye point (SE) 7–10 times while repeating the phrase: "But I'm feeling so stressed . . . There is so much going on . . ."
- Tap the under eye point (UE) 7–10 times while repeating the phrase: "I can't do it all . . . It's never going to work . . ."
- Tap the under nose point (UN) 7–10 times while repeating the phrase: "It's just too much . . . I can't handle it all . . ."
- Tap the chin point (CH) 7–10 times while repeating the phrase: "I'm really worried . . ."
- Tap the collarbone point (CB) 7–10 times while repeating the phrase: "What if I can't do it . . . What if I fail . . ."
- Tap the under arm point (UA) 7–10 times while repeating the phrase: "This stress in my body . . ."
- Tap the top of head point (TH) 7–10 times while repeating the phrase: "This remaining stress . . ."

Round 3:

- Tap the eyebrow point (EB) 7–10 times while repeating the phrase: "Even though I still have some stress, I know I can get some relief."
- Tap the side of eye point (SE) 7–10 times while repeating the phrase: "I choose to let go of my stress . . . Just for right now . . ."
- Tap the under eye point (UE) 7–10 times while repeating the phrase: "I'm breathing more fully . . ."
- Tap the under nose point (UN) 7–10 times while repeating the phrase: "My body is calming down . . ."
- Tap the chin point (CH) 7–10 times while repeating the phrase: "This remaining stress . . ."
- Tap the collarbone point (CB) 7–10 times while repeating the phrase: "What if it could calm down . . . That would be nice . . ."
- Tap the under arm point (UA) 7–10 times while repeating the phrase: "What if I could think more clearly . . . That would be great . . ."
- Tap the top of head point (TH) 7–10 times while repeating the phrase: "What if it was safe to relax . . . I am safe . . ."

Round 4:

- Tap the eyebrow point (EB) 7–10 times while repeating the phrase: "Even though I'm still a little stressed, I feel much better than I did . . ."
- Tap the side of eye point (SE) 7–10 times while repeating the phrase: "I understand and forgive myself for getting stressed . . ."
- Tap the under eye point (UE) 7–10 times while repeating the phrase: "With so much going on . . . Of course I got overwhelmed . . ."
- Tap the under nose point (UN) 7–10 times while repeating the phrase: "Feeling more in control now . . ."

- Tap the chin point (CH) 7–10 times while repeating the phrase: "I can figure this out . . ."
- Tap the collarbone point (CB) 7–10 times while repeating the phrase: "Being calm and confident . . ."
- Tap the under arm point (UA) 7–10 times while repeating the phrase: "Feeling grounded and supported . . ."
- Tap the top of head point (TH) 7–10 times while repeating the phrase: "Feeling calm and relaxed in this moment . . ."
- And gently stop tapping. Take a slow, deep breath.
- Notice the effects of tapping on the specific issue. Reassess the intensity level. How intense does "stress" feel to you now? Rate the intensity on a scale of 0–10.
- Take a few sips of water.
- If your intensity is still higher than you'd like, you can restart from Round 1 and keep repeating until the intensity decreases to 0. Please adjust the phrases as appropriate based on how you are feeling.

w that you have experienced the benefits, you might be even more rigued about this method. There are many scientific studies (over 275 peer-iewed, published studies as of this book's publication) that validate the cacy of EFT.

e of the most important benefits shown is that EFT intervention nificantly lowers cortisol levels according to Church et al. Research from ch et al. has shown that EFT can be helpful for many different conditions, luding specific phobias, anxiety, depression, pain, weight control, and letic performance. Again, EFT is another powerful tool to add to your lbox, but does not necessarily replace any conventional medical treatment. nsult your medical provider before making any specific changes to your imen.

COMMON QUESTIONS:

1) How long do the benefits last?

In order for EFT to be effective, the concern must be specific. Hence the importance of tweaking the phrases as appropriate to your situation. After a round of tapping, most people will feel some level of relief. The duration of this relief depends on how significant the original issue was. If it's something that has been ongoing for many years, it will most likely recur and require regular tapping practice. The good news is that as you continue to tap, you are creating your own sense of safety and removing the previous fear-based patterns. As you continue to uncover more patterns and "clear" them with EFT, the benefits will last longer.

2) Which side should I use? One or both sides?

The simple answer is it doesn't matter. Some people tap with both hands, some people tap with one. Use whichever one feels good to you.

3) How often should I tap?

As often as you'd like! It's a quick way to calm the system down, though of course you might not want to tap on your face when you're on Zoom in front of a team of fifteen . . .

4) I'm not sure I'm tapping the right points. It doesn't seem to be working for me?

Make sure to watch my video (scan the QR code!) so you can see me demonstrate tapping for you. You can use three fingers to increase your chances that you are hitting the appropriate points. And you might want to try increasing the pressure/force, but don't bruise yourself. And lastly, make sure you are drinking water and staying hydrated! Have a big glass of water and try again. The body needs water to function well (we are made up of 70% water, remember?) and when you're dehydrated, things don't work as well.

5) What am I supposed to feel during the process? What are these sensations

It is normal to experience sensations while tapping. Sensations such as warmth, tingling, blood flow, light, pulsations, and so on. Because tapping is stimulating the meridians connected to the brain and nervous system, the body responds by releasing chemicals that help you de-stress and let go of any stuck or unwanted energy. It may feel weird initially, but know that sensations are simply the body's way of communicating with you and will not kill you. You may notice more sensations the more you tap and open yourself up to the experience. Bring in the mindfulness principles of non-striving and non-judgment and allow yourself to experience what is.

QUESTIONS

1. Did EFT help improve my issue? By how much?
2. What issue(s) do I experience regularly?
3. When and where can I use EFT in my life?

PART IV

CONFIDENCE

The difference between ordinary and extraordinary is that something extra.

As a lifelong perfectionist, I was terrified of making a mistake and being a failure. I was afraid of being judged. Until I realized I was my own worst critic.

In this section, you will gain awareness and learn key processes to develop a strong sense of self-belief so that you don't hold yourself back.

You are meant to shine.

CHAPTER 7

THOUGHT WORK

"Whether you think you can or you think you can't
—you're right." —Henry Ford

w that you're feeling calm and grounded, I want to introduce you to
ught work—the process of looking at your thoughts and beliefs to change
r mindset. Learning to manage your mind is one of the most powerful
ls you can have when it comes to becoming confident and transforming
r life. Because how we see ourselves determines how we show up. When I
uss coaching, I see it as a way to look at your own mind and increase your
reness of what's going on.

member the conscious/subconscious mind iceberg from Chapter 2?
ching is one of the best ways to increase your conscious awareness by
ging parts of the submerged (subconscious) iceberg to the surface.

w, what is coaching, exactly? It's a supportive process where you work with
ide to identify your obstacles and challenges, and then learn tools to get
them with ease. There are coaches in many different fields, from business
elationships, life, health, and more. There are also more and more
ialized niches every day.

And yes, while it is *much* easier to work with a coach, it is possible do thought work by yourself, and I will guide you through this.

First, I want you to recognize that a belief is simply a thought you've thought over and over and over again. And a thought is simply words pieced together by your brain.

Sounds simple, right? So what does this mean?

It means that you are *not* your thoughts.

HINT: You are the observer of your thoughts.

This is empowering because it means you are capable of choosing your own thoughts and creating new beliefs.

And tying this back to a mindfulness practice, I want you to recognize that the circumstances and situations we are in are actually neutral. They just are. But we have our own thoughts about them.

Our thoughts serve as a filter, and thanks to this filtered lens, we develop certain feelings about certain circumstances and situations. And based on the feelings we have, we decide to act and behave in certain ways. Or *not* do certain things. And then we get certain results in our life.

This is demonstrated in the Model framework tool in Figure 7.1. It was created by Brooke Castillo, founder of the Life Coach School. You can use this tool to gain new insights, solve problems, and create new results in your life.

THE MODEL

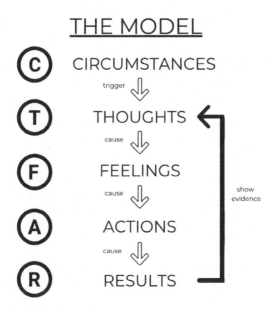

Figure 7.1: The Model

Here's an example to demonstrate this framework.

Right now it's 2022 and we are in a pandemic. This is a circumstance or situation we're in that is neutral. Okay, I know it's hard to think of it as neutral, but notice what reaction came up when I brought up the pandemic. Was it negative or positive for you?

Most of the time, I find that people are frustrated or tired of the pandemic. And they think the problem is the pandemic. *If only it was gone, if only life could go back to normal, if only I could travel again . . .*

But they actually skipped a step. It's actually what you *think* about the pandemic that is causing you to feel a certain way. So perhaps you have thoughts like, *These restrictions suck because I can't travel anymore* or *I can't see my family . . .* These thoughts are the root cause of you feeling negative or frustrated. Because the pandemic impacts everyone differently. Not everyone has the same thoughts.

Now, when you're feeling negative or frustrated, how do you behave? You're probably going to spend time doing things you wouldn't otherwise. Maybe you'll spend hours bingeing Netflix or have an extra glass of wine because what else is there to do at home . . . And then the result you get is that you've wasted more time and didn't do the work you're supposed to do. Or maybe you've gained some pandemic weight from all the drinking and snacking and whatever.

In contrast, let's take the same circumstance: the pandemic. And instead of complaining, what if you had a different thought? One like, *It's so nice not having to commute to work.* With this thought, you might be feeling grateful and excited to be able to have the flexibility to work from home. And when you're feeling grateful and excited, you're probably not going to sit on the couch for hours and waste time scrolling through social media. Instead, you'll probably do things that are really fulfilling, rewarding, and productive. As a result, you'll get more things done and have more time to enjoy your life.

Do you see how powerful our thoughts are? It really comes down to mindset. And the key is to be a non-judgmental observer of your thoughts. When you can catch yourself having unproductive thoughts leading you down a rabbit hole of negativity and stress, you can interrupt that pathway and choose new thoughts instead. Thoughts that will lead you to your desired feeling and outcome. To creating a better life for yourself.

Yes, you are that powerful. You are not stuck. You can change your life. Starting today.

EXERCISE: THE MODEL

Grab a piece of pen and paper. Write out the following letters vertically:

C: _____

T: _____

F: _____

A: _____

R: _____

- Think back to a recent time when you weren't feeling good. Write the feeling out next to F.

- What was the situation you were in? Write this circumstance out next to C. Remember, circumstances are facts that everyone agrees on and can be proven in a court of law.

- How did the circumstance trigger your discomfort? What were your thoughts surrounding the situation? Write your thoughts next to T.

- When you weren't feeling good, notice what you decided to do or not do. Write your actions next to A.

- Based on your behaviors, what ultimately happened? Write out your results next to R.

How was this exercise? What insights did you gain? Continue to use the Model tool regularly to gain awareness of your thoughts and actions.

You can also start with any letter and work backward or forward. As an example, if you want to build confidence surrounding a situation or circumstance, put *confidence* in the F line and ask yourself what thoughts you have to believe about the circumstance to lead to the feeling of confidence.

Consider thoughts like *I know what to do* or *This is so easy*. And when you're feeling confident, notice what actions you take or don't take. Do you procrastinate? Do you worry? Or do you get out there and get things done? And when you're taking action toward your dreams, what's the ultimate result? Are you closer to what you desire? You got this!

When we ask ourselves questions about our old beliefs and choose to let go of those that aren't serving us, we are rewiring our brain. We are making new nerve connections.

This is a practice that gets easier over time. Don't ever say it's too late.

The best time to plant a tree was twenty years ago, but the next best time is now.

There are many studies, including one from Dyrbye et al., showing how coaching has helped physicians recover from burnout and improved their resilience and quality of life. A study from McGovern et al. also showed Fortune 1000 executives experienced improved working relationships, job satisfaction, productivity, and profitability through working with a coach.

Coaching helps you unlearn your old patterns and release "limiting beliefs." These are stories you've been telling yourself about why things haven't been working out. Beliefs like *I can't do this, I'm not good enough, I don't know how* . . . No matter what stories you've been telling yourself, I want you to know that they don't have to be your reality moving forward.

you know, our brains are lazy. They prefer to be on autopilot to be
1fortable and conserve energy. They want you to stay in the comfort zone.
: if you want to live an amazing life full of purpose and fulfillment, it's
ng to require you to grow and expand. To step out of your comfort zone.
ause everything you want is right *outside*, as you see in Figure 7.2.

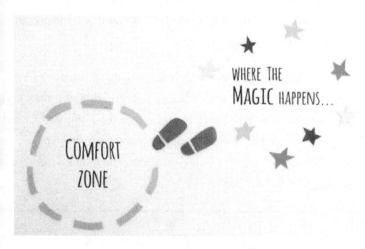

Figure 7.2: Outside the Comfort Zone

ou keep thinking the same thoughts and beliefs you've had, there will never
any breakthroughs. And before you start judging yourself, *stop*.

nember, you don't know what you don't know. When you know better,
do better.

rt from the Model, I would like to share another awareness tool called the
ought Download. This brain dump offers you an opportunity to become
observer of your thoughts. Let's try it out now.

EXERCISE: THOUGHT DOWNLOAD

Grab a pen and paper. Set a timer for five minutes and wri[te] down all the thoughts in your brain. Think about it like dumping o[ut] all of your thoughts and downloading them onto the paper. Resist th[e] urge to organize and make a "to-do list" but simply write everythin[g] out, without filter or judgment.

Okay, time's up. Do a quick assessment of what you wrot[e.] What's the overall theme? Is there a certain thought that kee[ps] repeating itself? You're welcome to plug it into the T line in the Mod[el] framework to identify how it impacts your feelings, actions, an[d] results. If you're ready to change, pick one thought that is causin[g] distress and let's dismantle it.

If you are like most people, many of the thoughts you wrote down [are] probably negative in nature. Is it any wonder why you don't feel good?

The subconscious is constantly replaying these same thoughts a[nd] strengthening the pathways. You must learn to break this cycle. You have [to] vigilantly monitor what's going on in your brain throughout the day so t[hat] it doesn't remain your reality.

And you might be wondering what to do about the negative thoughts n[ow] that you're aware of them. Proceed to the next exercise for my process [to] dismantle your thoughts. Think of your existing thoughts as a tangled bal[l of] yarn, creating a lot of distress and using up your precious energy. Through [the] dismantling process, you will pull one or multiple strings out to untangl[e,] and then before you know it, you will experience the satisfaction of the lo[ose] and untangled yarn to use as you'd like!

EXERCISE: THOUGHT DISMANTLING PROCESS

- Notice a recurring thought you have that's limiting your progress. Write it out on paper.

- Look at a thought on paper. Remind yourself that you are *not* the thought. You are simply the observer of the thought.

- Notice if the thought is making you feel a certain way, especially if it's a "negative" feeling. Acknowledge that you have feelings about and from this thought. Be in a state of non-judgment and non-striving. (Review Chapter 3 for definitions and principles of mindfulness).

- Take a few breaths to ground and get into the present moment. Notice the sensations in your body. Describe the sensations if you can. Allow them to be there. It will not kill you. Remember that they're simply trying to send you a message.

- Ask yourself the following questions:
  - Is the thought the absolute truth? (*Note*: It may feel true to you, but *truth* means it's a universal fact and true to everyone.)
  - Who am I when I am attached to this thought? How do I act?
  - What is believing this thought costing me?
  - Can I find a stress-free reason to keep this thought?
  - Who would I be without this thought?

- Make a decision. Choose whether you want to keep or trash the thought.

- Take one small action that reinforces your decision (e.g., *I am going to stop complaining for an hour and see how I feel*).

So often, we keep repeating the same thoughts over and over without pausing to question.

Every time we think the same thought, we are strengthening the nerve connections and making it a more deeply ingrained belief. If you keep thinking the thought *I have so much to do*, wouldn't it make sense why you are constantly feeling overwhelmed?

Now you might be saying, "But it's true, I *do* have a lot to do." And yes, you might have a lot going on. However, remember that it is your thoughts about your circumstance that dictate your feelings, actions, and eventual results.

What if you had the same number of things on your to-do list but instead thought, *I can handle this* or *This is going to be so easy*? How would that feel instead? Would you be more inspired and motivated to get through everything?

Now, you can spend hours coaching yourself all day, but the reason that having a coach is invaluable is because they can offer you a different perspective quickly and save you from making mistakes and wasting unnecessary time and energy.

Plus, you have someone to cheer you on, keep you accountable, and guide you along the way.

Imagine yourself in a foreign country, driving your rental car, trying to find a tourist destination while paying attention to all the speeding motorists and meandering taxi cabs—and then you accidentally run a red light and almost get into an accident. *Oops.*

Now, visualize having a local tour guide (a.k.a. coach) sitting in the car with you, calmly directing you to your destination and also pointing out blind spots to watch out for along the way. Oh, and you also get to hear funny jokes, learn nteresting facts, and take scenic shortcuts along the way. Which trip would ou rather take? Which one would be more fun?

This is why I love working with a coach: so I can avoid making mistakes I wouldn't have otherwise. And yes, coaching can be an investment. But through coaching, you will learn tools and skills that will serve you for the rest of your life. Isn't your well-being worth it?

QUESTIONS

1. What are the top three feelings I experience on a regular basis? What are the thoughts that cause those feelings?
2. What are the top three feelings I would *rather* experience instead? What are the thoughts that would cause these feelings?
3. When can I find the time and space to practice thought work in my life?

CHAPTER 8

VISUALIZATION & INTENTIONS

"Everything you can imagine is real." —Pablo Picasso

you know that the brain can't tell the difference between what's real and
t's imaginary? Visualization is the technique of using your imagination to
te what you want in your life. There is nothing strange, unusual, scary, or
risome about visualization. You are already using it every day without
izing.

en you think about confidence and self-belief, it's crucial to embody and
ome the version of you who *already* has what you want. Visualization is a
skill to develop in order to successfully transform.

es it really work? There are many studies demonstrating its effectiveness,
uding one by Ranganathan et al., which showed that participants were able
ain finger and arm muscle strength through visualization practices.

ause the subconscious is the one in control of running our daily lives, the
p-rooted negative beliefs that are programmed into our subconscious
tinue to guide our behavior without our conscious awareness or
ement. So we unconsciously continue to expect and imagine the same
itations, difficulties, and problems that we already have in our lives.

The good news is now that you understand how it works, you can use y‹ natural imagination in a more effective manner to create what you *tr* want—love, prosperity, inner peace, success, health, fulfillment, harmony whatever you desire!

Imagination is the ability to create a new idea, feeling, or mental image. O‹ you create a clear picture, idea, or feeling, you continue to focus on it regul‹ . . . until it becomes your reality.

I know it might seem too good to be true. It's like, if all I needed was imagine I was a millionaire, why hasn't it happened yet?! Maybe you're alre‹ repeating affirmations eighteen times a day. You created a vision board. Y‹ meditate regularly. You "believe." *But it doesn't work!* This is why you can o‹ trust things that are backed with scientific studies!

The problem is this: You may have the thought or idea, but you haven't lea‹ into the feelings to bring the idea into actual, physical form.

Think of yourself as an architect designing a house. You spend hours a‹ hours sketching out this beautiful blueprint. It's perfect! But you don't kn‹ the actual budget or schedule timeline. You don't follow up with the ow‹ and construction team. And if you do that, even the most perfect house ‹ paper will never become a real house in real life. The idea and blueprints v‹ never become a reality. Is that what you really want? What a waste of y‹ talents!

The key is to lean into the feelings. You have to connect your mind and b‹ in order to have this actualize.

HINT: When you are dreaming of a better life and future, you have ‹ reinvent yourself.

I see reinvention as a process to change our old patterns and evolve into a better version of ourselves. But it can be challenging when we are stuck in our old patterns and limitations.

So, what's the process? Before you get too excited, you need a roadmap. It's like you're ready to go somewhere, so you jump into your car and just start driving. Except you have no idea where you're going. You didn't identify a destination or put it in your GPS, so after a while, you're just driving around to nowhere. Wasting gas, time, and energy. To save you the trouble, here's a more efficient way instead.

The first step is to pause with mindfulness and awareness. Give yourself a destination so you know where you're headed. Then you can put it into your GPS and get where you want to go with ease.

This is where intentions come in. Think of intentions as an instruction manual that helps you decide on the destination you want to drive to so that you can enter it into your car's GPS and get directions. I see intentions as a guiding principle for *who* you want to be and *how* you want to act.

Intentions are *not* the same as a goal, however. A goal is something you want to achieve and accomplish in the future. You need *both* intentions and goals to be successful, but you start with intentions to have the big-picture direction, and then you execute with goals.

Intentions are also emotion-driven, connecting to the body and feelings, while goals are more action-driven, connecting to the mind and thoughts. We often only think about setting goals and forget that if we're not connected to the big picture, the emotions, and the *why*, we actually end up not wanting to achieve our goals.

Have you ever procrastinated on something? Maybe you said yes to an event or project because you thought it was what you "should" do. But you actually didn't want to do it, and instead, you ended up scrolling social media, bingeing on Netflix, or eating cookies when you weren't even hungry! I know I've been guilty of this, so that's why I don't want you to deal with it too.

But procrastination is not just from lack of motivation. I know you want to do well and be productive. Procrastinating is usually the action we take when we feel overwhelmed or don't feel good. Remember the coaching Model from Chapter 7 and how our actions stem from our feelings? And our feelings come from our thoughts about a circumstance? So, the key is to learn how to manage our thoughts and beliefs.

The proposed goal most likely wasn't fully aligned with your true vision and intentions, so you had doubts or concerns about it (e.g. negative thoughts). And from these thoughts, you developed negative feelings surrounding it, making it hard to find that internal motivation and drive to take action and get the results (e.g. goal completion) you're looking for.

Review Table 8.1 below for details between an intention and a goal.

Table 8.1 Intention and Goal Differences

	Intention	Goal
Definition	**Guiding principle for WHO you want to be** and how you want to show up in life	Something **you want to achieve/accomplish** in the future
Approach	• Emotion-driven • Big-picture vision, "being" • "What do I want my purpose to be this year?"	• Action-driven • To-do list, "doing" • "What are the steps I need to take to make this happen?"

I also want to share the most common goal-setting mistakes I see in clients who have been feeling stuck or having trouble achieving the results they want. You may see yourself in one or more of these . . .

COMMON GOAL-SETTING MISTAKES

1. You set uninspiring goals. You set goals because you think you "should" achieve them, but they don't actually feel exciting or good to you.

2. You don't believe the goals are attainable or possible for you. A lot of times we have big dreams and ideas, but if we don't actually connect with our vision and intentions, our subconscious will prevent us from moving forward.

3. You don't take time to reflect on past goals and experiences. History keeps repeating itself because you haven't learned the lesson yet and you keep repeating the same patterns and mistakes. As I like to say, you get either the results you wanted or the lessons you needed.

4. You give yourself too many goals. You've caught "shiny object syndrome" and it's too overwhelming for your system to handle, so you can't even do one well.

And before we get into creating our vision and setting intentions so they come true, we have to first clear the air and let go of the past. It's like you finally get the keys to the house of your dreams, ready to move in all your amazing new furniture . . .

But when you open the door, your heart sinks immediately because you see that the previous owner didn't remove any of their stuff! The garage is packed with junk, the furniture and decor are definitely not your style, plus there seems to be a weird smell coming from somewhere . . . You have no room to bring your stuff in and start a better life, right? This is why it's so important to let go of the past and clear away what's not serving you so that you can reinvent yourself.

Know that our past can often keep us stuck because it's familiar to us. It feels comfortable and safe. And you already know that the brain is all about safety and survival. So even if it doesn't make us super happy or help us reach our highest good, we tend to stay attached and tethered to it. This may apply to certain beliefs, ideas, people, events, and traumas. It's very much tied to our identity. We don't want to let go because it's scary to change and try something new.

The good news is I have developed an easy, three-step process based in mindfulness to help you let go of what's not serving you. Let's use the example of wanting to get a promotion to make a bigger impact in your organization.

EXERCISE: LETTING GO PROCESS

1) Stop.

First acknowledge what is and notice the now.

Notice when you're worrying or stressing about whether you're doing the right thing, judging how your performance has been, or reminiscing about all the good times and bad, when you were too nervous to speak up in a big meeting or whatever . . . Just *notice* where your thoughts go without judgment or shame.

You can do this by taking a simple, cleansing breath, inhaling through your nose and exhaling through your open mouth . . . Take a moment to get into your body again.

2) Ask.

Be curious and find out why this past event or issue keeps coming up for you.

Ask yourself, "What do I gain by holding onto this story?" Even though it seems unhelpful to keep judging or sabotaging yourself, there's usually some type of gain or benefit to it. Maybe it means you don't have to create and give presentations because it's a lot of work (and nobody has time for that!).

It's interesting to notice that there usually is a reason to our madness.

3) Choose.
Last step is to choose, knowing that you always get to choose. You can make your own decision and take action from it.

Remember, you are making a decision by *not* making a decision. Once you understand the reason behind holding onto your story, you can decide what to do next.

If you're done, willing, and ready to let go of this version of you that doesn't want to speak in public, you can make a new commitment. Put your hand on your chest, close your eyes, say to yourself: "I commit to letting go." See yourself letting go of this past, cutting all cords and ties, like releasing a balloon into the sky, feeling lighter after.

ou want a powerful guided meditation to let go of and cut ties to your past, ke sure to download my free gift for you here!

cindytsaimd.com/somuchbetterbookgift

w that you've let go, you have cleared space to welcome in the good. In : next exercise, we can focus on setting intentions that work through 1alization.

EXERCISE: INTENTION SETTING & VISUALIZATION PROCES

1) Identify your desire.
This can be big or small. Imagine you have a magic wand an everything is possible—what would you like to come true? Focus o the *feeling* you want to experience. For example, do you want to fe happy? Peaceful? Loved? Excited? Think about the feeling you wa to experience.

2) Get clear on *who* you have to be.
Goals are about doing while intentions are about *being*. Whe you focus on who you need to *be* to achieve this goal, the doir becomes easier. For example, if you want to have a successful busines who is this version of you who already *has* a successful busines Think about . . .

> What qualities does this version of you have?
> What do they believe?
> What do they see?
> What do they hear?
> What do they smell?
> What do they feel?
> What do they do?
> What's the surrounding environment like?

Remember, *who* before *how*. When you know the *who*, the *ho* becomes much easier, because you'll know the exact things to do get to where you want to go.

3) Identify and remove any limiting beliefs and stories that you have Remember we have to let go of our past and clear space in order t welcome in the good. When you don't believe you can achieve accomplish what you want, you *must* reframe your mindset to ensu

your beliefs align with your desire. Maybe you need to let go of the idea *I'm not a business person. I don't like selling. I hate being on social media.* Practice using the tools mentioned in Chapter 7 on thought work to build your confidence.

4) Practice, practice, *practice*!

This is an *active* process because you actually have to take *action* in order for intentions to come true. It's not like you write them down and they magically come true. It's a process that takes practice and commitment. But before you get discouraged, don't confuse process with slow. I have seen things turn around very quickly when people are able to fully lean into the "being" mentioned in Step 2. Keep practicing, reinforcing, reminding yourself of what you need to believe, feel, and do so that it becomes your reality. Focus on all your wins and evidence of how things *are* already working. Every little bit counts!

Okay, did you do the practice? How did it feel?

I can't emphasize enough the importance of staying focused. You can have everything you want, but don't go after everything all at once, because that's the surest way to overwhelm and burnout. Don't have more than three intentions at once. It's more powerful to be laser-focused on one and have it come true more quickly than expected than it is to balance three intentions and get disappointed because you end up delayed by months.

You are already on your way. I believe in you.

QUESTIONS

1. Think about the last goal I didn't accomplish. What was the reason why?

2. What are my one to two intentions for the next ninety days?

3. Visualize my intentions coming true. How can I describe this future reality as if it were already here? Be as detailed as possible so that a stranger could easily draw out the vision!

PART V

CURIOSITY

How much fun do you have every day?

When you are doing the same thing every day, it's easy to lose your sense of curiosity. There is also a tendency to disconnect and be on autopilot because it's easy. You become a cog in the wheel, and before you know it, years have gone by. Curiosity and having a beginner's mind are one of the key principles of mindfulness. It's important to stay present, or else you lose sight of all the fun!

Humans are creative beings.

We are gifted with the talents and skills to transform the world.

This section will reveal some of my favorite techniques to help you access your inner wisdom now. Anything is possible.

CHAPTER 9

JOURNALING

"The quality of your life is determined by the quality of the questions you ask." —Tony Robbins

you know that journaling is a great way to build your curiosity muscle practice mindfulness? There are different ways to journal, but it helps to pen your focus, direct your attention to the present moment, and can ease positive thoughts and decrease negative thoughts.

dies have shown the best way to process your emotions is through either ing or speaking. Stice et al. showed that journaling can reduce depression, le Goodman et al. showed that journaling can reduce anxiety symptoms. also a great way to boost immune function, as shown by Baikie et al.

rnaling is a great writing tool that helps get your thoughts and feelings paper. You uncover what you're feeling and going through. It's amazing much insight you get when you can see your thoughts (as you have seen ugh the Thought Download tool in Chapter 7!)

ie people find journaling tedious, but I want to remind you that you get hoose. You get to design and do it however you want. Every day. Every k. Every month. Whatever works for you. Don't overthink it.

You don't need to get the $30 journal. Make it simple. Make it fun. Play m music. Go sit somewhere quiet where you won't be interrupted. Practice so breathing techniques from Chapter 5. Remember you can create your o state of calm.

HINT: Honor yourself.

In case you're wondering, there is something to be said about writing it hand versus typing on the computer. I usually recommend writing things because it helps the brain process information better, as shown by Muelle al.

Here are a few types of journaling practices I recommend you try in order build your curiosity muscle. Details for each are included below.

1. Gratitude Journaling
2. Reflective Journaling
3. Emotional Detox Journaling
4. Freewrite Journaling

EXERCISE: GRATITUDE JOURNALING

Gratitude journaling is one of the best tools to help you feel better.

Every morning or evening, think of three things you are grateful for and write them down. I recommend you to come up with different things every day. This practice will allow you to stretch and grow. To focus on what you do have.

Give thanks for *everything* in your life. Specifically and exactly the way they are. Even if your preference is for it to be different. Remember, curiosity is about being open and in wonder. It's hard to be in awe when you are full of judgment. When you are constantly wanting things to be different, you are caught up in your own stories. Replaying regrets from the past. Experiencing worries and projections about the future. Neither one serves you. Neither one is real. The only real moment you have is the present. The now.

In my own experience and through working with many clients, I have seen the magic that happens when you are in a state of gratitude. You attract more into your life. It sounds counterintuitive, but when you are feeling blissful and happy to be alive, regardless of how things are, more good things come your way. I also urge you to pause after each item of gratitude. Really pay attention to how it makes you feel. Embody and experience it. Feel it in your body. What *does* it feel like when you are grateful to have a roof over your head and clothes to wear?

Remember, the more you do it, the easier it gets. You will train your brain to focus on all the things that *are* working. Toggle your brain's search engine filter to only look for success, not failure. Shift your perception from what you don't have to what you *do*. This increases your sense of abundance to attract more abundance, in return.

As you know by now the power of intentions, I find it helpful to start and end the day with Reflective Journaling prompts as below.

<u>EXERCISE: REFLECTIVE JOURNALING</u>

Sometimes it's easier when we have prompts to follow and get us into a reflective state. Here are some of my favorite journal prompts, which I invite you to try.

START OF DAY
<u>Set Your Day Up for Success</u>
What am I looking forward to?
What might challenge me?
What will I do if I feel stressed/anxious?
If I could live this day over again, what would I do differently?
What is the most important thing I need to do?
This is how I'll make today great . . .
What's my intention for the day?
How do I want to feel today?
What is something I'm going to do for myself today?

EXERCISE: REFLECTIVE JOURNALING

END OF DAY
<u>Three Things Today</u>

> What are three things that challenged me?
>
> What are three events that made me feel productive?
>
> What are three wonderful things I heard?
>
> What are three experiences that made me feel brave?
>
> What are three things I learned?
>
> What are three beautiful things I saw?
>
> What are three ways I felt loved?
>
> What are three things that made me smile?
>
> Come up with your own!

<u>Reflections</u>

> What great things did I experience today?
>
> What am I proud of myself for?
>
> What will I do differently tomorrow?
>
> What am I grateful for?
>
> What was my good deed today?
>
> The funniest thing I heard today was . . .
>
> Something that bothered me was . . .
>
> What did I learn today?

Now, some people like to refer back to their past journals to review and reflect. However, if you're having a bad day, it's important to process the negativity and release it so it doesn't stay stuck and weigh you down. To do this, I want you to do Emotional Detox Journaling so that you can feel better. Your writing will be destroyed when it is complete. No one ever reads it, not even you.

EXERCISE: EMOTIONAL DETOX JOURNALING

Create a space and time where you will not be interrupted and have plenty of paper and a pen. First state your intention: "My intention is to clear, release, and let go of anything that no longer serves me." Give yourself permission to be completely honest, brutal, expressive, and passionate about whatever comes forward for you to write.

Start writing. Whatever triggering event, painful experience, fear, grief, or sadness comes forward, just put it down on paper. If a body part hurts, give it a voice and write what it has to say. Whatever comes to mind, write it out. Don't hold back. This is an emotional and mental cleanse. Time to let it all out. *You cannot do this wrong.* Don't worry about dotting every *i* and crossing every *t*. You don't need to write in complete sentences. Your handwriting does not need to be legible. It does not matter what or how you are writing. You are clearing your subconscious mind. Trust that whatever is coming up and out is exactly what needs to be released. Scribbling works too. Keep going.

The more you purge, the better you will feel. The only rule is . . . do *not* read over what you wrote! You will know when you are finished because the energy will run out. You can give it a few minutes to see if anything more comes out.

Now for the fun part! Shred or burn your papers. If neither option is available to you, simply rip the paper up and throw it away where it cannot be found. Get it out of your space and home. Joyfully watch your papers be destroyed and discarded.

! Bravo! Acknowledge yourself for doing this work. This is part of your -care. It takes willingness and courage to let go and release unwanted bage from your consciousness. We're so used to holding everything in and ping it together, but you don't have to!

w, make sure you fill your space with positive energy. Thoughts and rmations of self-appreciation, forgiveness, gratitude, and love. You may feel ter, freer, or even tired and drained. No matter what you feel, it's okay. t and relax. Drink water. Do not try to recall what you wrote. If you still e negative or painful thoughts, repeat this process over again. You should better after.

tly, try out the Freewrite Journaling practice to check in with yourself. tructions as below.

XERCISE: FREEWRITE JOURNALING

If you are the type who likes to do what you want, I invite you to set some time for freewriting. Simply sit and allow yourself to write whatever comes up. Anything that has come up for you recently. Anything that's on your mind. How you're feeling. The good and the bad. Allow everything to come through. Be open. Enjoy the moment with yourself. Some people like to do this on a regular basis, whether it's every week or every month, and let it serve as a time machine of memories to refer back to. Whatever works for you.

JESTIONS

1. Which journaling practice did I enjoy? Why?
2. When is a good time for me to journal?
3. Do I have resistance toward journaling? Why?

CHAPTER 10

CREATIVITY & FUN

"An essential aspect of creativity is not being afraid to fail." —Edwin Land

Are you creative?

I never thought I was creative. I always thought being creative was reserved for the artists and designers. The ones with artistic talent. Not someone who draws stick figures and does paint-by-numbers kits (a.k.a. me).

But as I continued my journey of reconnecting with myself, I found that I was indeed a creative person. I broadened my definition of creativity to the ability to develop and produce original work in any form. *Any* form.

Creativity is closely related to curiosity, as you must be willing to explore and try new things. To experiment. To fail. To keep going.

As a game, look at Figure 10.1 and see if you can guess which one was drawn by a child versus a famous abstract expressionist. (Answer revealed at end of chapter.)

Figure 10.1: Abstract Artwork

Kids are gifted with an abundance of creativity. They are filled with curiosity, playfulness, fun, and joy.

However, as we grow older, we learn that the adult world is not a safe place for children. We suffered wounds and hurt as children that often linger and stay with us through our adult lives. The growing kid then buries this delightful child spirit underground—our so-called "inner child."

The term *inner child* was first coined by psychologist Carl Jung and represents the child-like aspect within our subconscious mind. While the inner child constantly tries to get our attention, we have forgotten how to listen and simply ignore our inner child. When the inner child is blocked, we are not able to fully express ourselves. We lose connection with who we really are and who we are meant to be.

Symptoms of a wounded inner child may include low self-esteem, fear of abandonment, inability to express and manage your emotions, fear of expressing needs and boundaries, trust issues, people-pleasing tendencies, and so on.

Through doing inner child work and healing, you can discover and release the repressed emotions holding you back, resolve unhelpful patterns, and reclaim your creativity and playfulness to have more fun in your life.

This book is not designed to be a substitute for the many wonderful resources available for inner child work but can serve as an introduction to explore this area if it is resonating with you.

One of the easiest ways to reconnect with your inner child is to bring in "play." Kids love to play, explore, and experiment with new ways of doing things. The inner child lives in our imagination. Observe children wherever possible. Watch what they do, listen to what they say. Be with them without judgment, without having to change them. They will teach you about your inner child, in case you have forgotten.

It is also important to start rebuilding trust with your inner child. Do activities that you enjoyed as a kid and treat them with respect, acceptance, open-mindedness, and love.

Allow your child to be a child. Let it draw and write like a child. Let it speak like a child. Create safety so that the child will want to come out and play again. Do the following exercise to start this process to reconnect with your inner child.

EXERCISE: MEET YOUR INNER CHILD

Materials: Paper with crayons or color pencils

Sit quietly and picture in your mind a beautiful place where you will visit with your inner child in your imagination. Make sure it is a safe and comfortable place. It might be out in nature, a beautiful park with trees and flowers, perhaps somewhere near the ocean or mountains. Or it could be a private, warm, cozy room with a dimly lit fireplace.

Close your eyes and take some breaths to ground first. Allow yourself to go to this beautiful place. In your imagination, see your inner child there, and spend a few moments with the child. Notice what the child is doing, what they look like, if they have anything to say to you. Have a conversation if they're willing. Take as long as you'd like.

Open your eyes and use your non-dominant hand to draw a picture of your inner child. Take your time and let this drawing unfold from your inner child. Do not plan it or try to picture the outcome in advance. It's normal to feel awkward and slow. Just be patient. This is your inner child speaking through pictures, communicating with you again.

As you are drawing, pause and notice your experience. Did you criticize yourself for the manner in which your child drew the picture? Did you relax and have fun allowing your inner child to be itself and draw in its own style?

Look at the finished drawing. How do you feel about it? What does the child in the picture seem to be saying to you? Are they happy or sad? On a separate piece of paper, use your dominant hand to write down any reactions or comments about the drawing. What insights did you gain?

I also see creativity as an opportunity to express yourself authentically. When I removed my perfectionist hat, I realized that there was so much possibility in the world. We are *all* creative beings. There are *so* many ideas waiting to come through into the real world. We only have to pay attention and *listen*.

As a high achiever, you may be prone to perfectionist tendencies like me. So I want you to give yourself permission to let things be messy. It's all going to be fine in the end. If it's not fine, then it's not the end.

are playing make-believe in a safe and controlled environment. Wouldn't
rather experiment here than be pushed out of a plane to skydive in the
world? (If you've done this before, kudos to you!) The more open and
ative you are, the more curiosity you will develop and the more enriching
e you will live.

l if you find it hard to give yourself permission . . . consider Figure 10.2 to
your official permission slip.

PERMISSION SLIP

To do nothing. To do something.
To say yes. To say no.
To be unproductive.
To feel happy. To feel sad.
To do what feels good for you.
To be YOU and ONLY YOU.

Figure 10.2: Permission Slip

important to note that when we are feeling stressed, it's harder to access
creativity and wisdom. According to Dinse et al., the stress hormone
isol blocks perceptual learning (which basically means being able to
ond to different stimuli based on our experiences and respond
ordingly, and the key to creativity and bringing ideas to life!), so this is why
may find it hard to be creative when you have twelve other things to get
n your to-do list.

access your creativity and wisdom, your system must believe that you are
place of safety. This is why we started Part III with the pillar of calm. If

you're about to be eaten by a bear, your brain wants you to run, not sit on grass staring at the sky identifying what animals the clouds resemble.

While it may seem weird to structure "blank space" in your schedule to creative, it trains your brain to relax and be open to ideas. It's akin to hav a blank canvas and a fully loaded paint palette, ready for a beaut masterpiece to emerge.

Schedule downtime to relax so that your brain can be creative and curio You may have heard or experienced that you get your best ideas in the show The brain provides the best ideas when it's relaxed, distracted, and releas the feel-good chemical dopamine. Showers are easy because they're a safe pl when we experience dopamine release, we're relaxed, and we're distracted a mindless activity.

It can also be helpful to spend time in nature and feel grounded and inspi by our surroundings. We forget that nature is our playground. Spend ti doing activities that light you up. The most important thing is to lean into *fun*. You are the one calling the shots.

HINT: You get to choose. Every single time.

<u>QUESTIONS</u>

1. What did I like to do for fun as a kid?
2. How can I be more creative in my every day?
3. How much fun/play time do I give myself every day?

ANSWER: The image on left was drawn by four-year-old Jack Pezanos while the image on right was drawn by abstract expressionist Hans Hoffm.

PART VI

NEXT STEPS

To know and not do, is to not know.

Congratulations! You now have more than
enough tools in your toolkit.

The question is, what are you going to do about it?

How can you make sure that you implement and
achieve the results you deserve?

CHAPTER 11

CONSISTENCY

"What you do today can improve all your tomorrows."
—*Ralph Marston*

This book has offered you many useful tools to support you on your journey, but the key to results is consistency. Ask yourself, on a scale of 1–10, how committed are you to living a better life? Why did you pick that specific number? If it's not a 10, what would make it a 10?

I know you lead a busy life and it can be hard to find time to do all the exercises. Here are some suggestions to set yourself up for success.

. Be honest.
Ask yourself how much time you have to realistically commit to your own growth and development. Do you tell yourself you "should" do this or that? *Stop should-ing over yourself.* It only leads to feelings of inadequacy, frustration and self-rejection. Remove the word *should* from your vocabulary. I mean it.

Do you notice yourself feeling better, with more calm, confidence, and curiosity in your life? Do you want to see how much better it can get? It's okay if things are busy right now, don't put yourself in any compromising situations.

HINT: You don't *have* to do anything, you *get* to.

The most important thing is to rebuild your connection and trust with yourself.

2. Be brave.
    I hope you know how much courage it takes to do this inner work. And how brave you are for stepping up and doing this. You are meant for more. I know it. Don't give up. Remember to allow and feel your feelings. Every feeling is simply a sensation in your body. Imagine being unafraid to feel any feeling—fear, anxiety, shame, rejection, guilt, sadness, embarrassment, pain, anything! What would that life look like?

3. Be patient.
    Remember that this is a process and we are all on our own journeys. Do not compare your beginning to someone else's ending. Every journey begins with a single step. You are exactly where you need to be right now. And you won't be here forever. *There* is not better than *here*. If you find yourself frustrated, stuck, and impatient, ask yourself why. What is the lesson here? How are things working out in your favor?

4. Find support.
    You are not meant to do this alone. Humans are social creatures who need connection. You can find support and accountability in local and online communities, organizations, books, podcasts, and more. You may feel isolated now, but you might be pleasantly surprised to hear that others are having very similar experiences to you. We are all human, after all.

And if you're someone who is going to be an inspiring success story, then you already know that investing in yourself is required. You know that you need a coach/mentor/guide so that you don't fail and waste time like everyone else.

ch out to me (**hello@cindytsaimd.com**) so I can direct you to the best
urces based on your situation! I'm here to help!

JESTIONS

1. Where do I need to be more honest with myself?
2. How can I be brave when things get uncomfortable?
3. Am I being patient, impatient, or complacent? What action(s) can I take to move forward?
4. What level of support do I need to ensure my success is inevitable?

CHAPTER 12

GRATITUDE

"Be thankful for what you have; you'll end up having more.
If you concentrate on what you don't have, you will never,
ever have enough." —Oprah Winfrey

People talk about the importance of gratitude, but practicing gratitude is often easier said than done.

You might be grateful when things are working out, when it's a beautiful day, or when you go on vacation. It's another story when you're stuck in horrendous traffic, when your teenager gives you attitude, or when there are fires to put out at work. I get it.

As I dove deep into my own healing and coaching work, I became aware of the pervasive lack and scarcity that was deeply ingrained in my subconscious. It may sound weird but that was my comfort zone. I was used to being driven by fear and resisted change. I was worried about things outside of my control and was constantly nervous about when the other shoe would drop. I thought I needed certain things or milestones to be happy and satisfied. I was focused on problems and everything that could go wrong. I was exhausted.

And then I learned about and shifted into the abundance mindset, and everything changed. I took control of my life, beliefs, and actions. I embraced risk and change, knowing that this is all for my higher good. I saw that there was more than enough to go around in the world for everybody! I gave generously and saw every problem as an opportunity for a solution. I focused on service and learning. I remembered my self-worth and stayed grounded in who I was. I showed up every day energized and excited to experience life.

If you have a tendency towards a scarcity mindset, I want you to know that you're not alone. The world is set up this way, rooted in so much fear, by default. Our brains want to help us survive! But the good news is now that you're aware, you can change things! It's like touching your hand to a hot stove—once you feel the pain, you immediately withdraw. You don't keep your hand on the stove for an hour to feel *more* pain, right?

So, are you ready for the secret to going from a scarcity mindset to an abundance mindset?

One word: Gratitude. Immense, deep gratitude.

HINT: Give thanks for *everything* in your life.

Specifically and exactly for the way they are, regardless of any preference for things to be different.

Yes, it can be challenging, but it's a practice, meaning it gets easier the more you do it. Try it out to see for yourself!

QUESTIONS

1. How does the scarcity mindset show up in my life? What would an abundance mindset look like?
2. What are thirty things I am grateful for today? Stretch to look for the silver linings.
3. Who am I grateful for today? How can I express my sincere gratitude toward them?

CONCLUSION

"Your time is limited, so don't waste it living someone else's life." —*Steve Jobs*

Wow! You did it!

You are well on your way toward becoming an inspiring success story. I am so honored to be a part of your journey and can't wait to see all the amazing things you are here to share.

MINT: Remember that you are enough, right now, just as you are.

As you reconnect and build trust with yourself through mastering calm, confidence, and curiosity, you will learn to accept and love yourself unconditionally.

When you love yourself unconditionally, you will take better care of yourself and feel better. When you feel better, you will be inspired and able to give more to others. When you readily share your love and compassion, you will make a big impact, create movements, and help the world become a better place for all.

If you haven't signed up for my free video training series to recap my Inspiring Success Story Method™, make sure to do it now by scanning the QR code below!

cindytsaimd.com/somuchbetterbookgift

Thank you for joining me on this very important mission. Sending you so much love and light!

PEARLS OF WISDOM

ly, here's a list of all the **HINTS** I've included in each chapter as aways.

- In order to enjoy life, you have to be present.
- We can't change what we don't know.
- Fear is not the same as danger.
- Nothing is good or bad. It just is.
- What if your success was inevitable?
- You are here on your journey.
- You are the observer of your thoughts.
- When you are dreaming of a better life and future, you have to reinvent yourself.
- Honor yourself.
- You get to choose. Every single time.
- You don't *have* to do anything, you *get* to.
- Give thanks for *everything* in your life.
- You are enough, right now, just as you are.

ich one is your favorite? Email me at <u>hello@cindytsaimd.com</u> to let me w!

REFERENCES

CHAPTER 1

Breines, Juliana G., and Serena Chen. "Self-Compassion Increases Self-Improvement Motivation." *Personality and Social Psychology Bulletin* 38, no. 9 (2012): 1133–43. https://doi.org/10.1177/0146167212445599.

Liao, Kelly Yu-Hsin, Graham B. Stead, and Chieh-Yu Liao. "Meta-Analysis of the Relation Between Self-Compassion and Self-Efficacy." *Mindfulness* 12, no. 8 (2021): 1878–91. https://doi.org/10.1007/s12671-021-01626-4.

Neff, Kristen. *Self-Compassion: The Proven Power of Being Kind to Yourself.* New York: HarperCollins, 2011.

CHAPTER 2

Breit, Sigrid, Aleksandra Kupferberg, Gerhard Rogler, and Gregor Hasler. "Vagus Nerve as Modulator of the Brain-Gut Axis in Psychiatric and Inflammatory Disorders." *Frontiers in Psychiatry* 9, no. 44 (2018). https://doi.org/10.3389/fpsyt.2018.00044.

Kihlstrom, John F. "The Psychological Unconscious and the Self." In *Novartis Foundation Symposia 174: Experimental and Theoretical Studies of Consciousness*, edited by Gregory R. Bock and Joan Marsh. 147–67. London: Ciba Foundation, 2007. https://doi.org/10.1002/9780470514412.ch8.

Reddan, Marianne Cumella, Tor Dessart Wager, and Daniela Schiller. "Attenuating Neural Threat Expression with Imagination." *Neuron*

100, no. 4 (2018): 994–1005.e4.
https://doi.org/10.1016/j.neuron.2018.10.047.

CHAPTER 5

Zaccaro, Andrea, Andrea Piarulli, Marco Laurino, Erika Garbella, Danilo
    Menicucci, Bruno Neri, and Angelo Gemignani. "How Breath-Control
    Can Change Your Life: A Systematic Review on Psycho-Physiological
    Correlates of Slow Breathing." *Frontiers in Human Neuroscience* 12
    (2018). https://doi.org/10.3389/fnhum.2018.00353.

CHAPTER 6

Bach, Donna, Gary Groesbeck, Peta Stapleton, Rebecca Sims, Katharina
    Blickheuser, Dawson Church. "Clinical EFT (Emotional Freedom
    Techniques) Improves Multiple Physiological Markers of Health."
    Journal of Evidence-Based Integrative Medicine 24 (2019).
    https://doi.org/10.1177/2515690x18823691.

Church, Dawson, Garret Young, Audrey J. Brooks. "The Effect of
    Emotional Freedom Techniques on Stress Biochemistry." *Journal of
    Nervous & Mental Disease* 200, no. 10 (2012): 891–96.
    https://doi.org/10.1097/nmd.0b013e31826b9fc1.

CHAPTER 7

Dyrbye, Liselotte N., Tait D. Shanafelt, Priscilla R. Gill, Daniel V. Satele,
    Colin P. West. "Effect of a Professional Coaching Intervention on the
    Well-Being and Distress of Physicians." *JAMA Internal Medicine* 179,
    no. 10 (2019): 1406–14.
    https://doi.org/10.1001/jamainternmed.2019.2425.

McGovern, Joy, Michael Lindemann, Monica Vergara, Stacey Murphy,
    Linda Barker, Rodney Warrenfeltz. "Maximizing the Impact of

Executive Coaching: Behavioral Change, Organizational Outcomes, and Return on Investment." *The Manchester Review* 6, no. 1 (2001): 1-9.

CHAPTER 8

Ranganathan, Vinoth K., Vlodek Siemionow, Jing Z. Liu, Vinod Sahgal, and Guang H. Yue. "From Mental Power to Muscle Power—Gaining Strength by Using the Mind." *Neuropsychologia* 42, no. 7 (2004): 944–56. https://doi.org/10.1016/j.neuropsychologia.2003.11.018.

CHAPTER 9

Baikie, Karen A., and Kay Wilhelm. "Emotional and Physical Health Benefits of Expressive Writing." *Advances in Psychiatric Treatment* 11, no. 5 (2005): 338–46. https://doi.org/10.1192/apt.11.5.338.

Goodman, Joely Tara, and Melissa Henry. "Reflective Journaling to Decrease Anxiety among Undergraduate Nursing Students in the Clinical Setting." *Journal of Nursing Education and Practice* 9, no. 5 (2019): 75. https://doi.org/10.5430/jnep.v9n5p75.

Mueller, Pam A., and Daniel M. Oppenheimer. "The Pen Is Mightier Than the Keyboard: Advantages of Longhand over Laptop Note Taking." *Psychological Science* 25, no. 6 (2014): 1159–68. https://doi.org/10.1177/0956797614524581.

Stice, Eric, Emily Burton, Sarah Kate Bearman, and Paul Rohde. "Randomized Trial of a Brief Depression Prevention Program: An Elusive Search for a Psychosocial Placebo Control Condition." *Behaviour Research and Therapy* 45, no. 5 (2007): 863–76. https://doi.org/10.1016/j.brat.2006.08.008.

CHAPTER 10

Dinse, Hubert R., J.C. Kattenstroth, M. Lenz, M. Tegenthoff, and O.T. Wolf. "The Stress Hormone Cortisol Blocks Perceptual Learning in Humans." *Psychoneuroendocrinology* 77 (2017): 63–67. https://doi.org/10.1016/j.psyneuen.2016.12.002.

ABOUT THE AUTHOR

dy Tsai, MD is a board-certified internal medicine physician turned
epreneur, mindfulness teacher, life coach, keynote speaker, and wellness
rt. She has always been passionate about self-development and loves
ing people live their true purpose and become the best they can be.

earned her BA and MS degrees from Johns Hopkins University and her
degree from Geisel School of Medicine at Dartmouth. As a primary care
sician, she saw the impacts of chronic stress on the body and wanted to do
e than just prescribe medications as a Band-Aid. Throughout her own
ing journey, she has explored and trained in a wide range of therapeutic
lalities and emphasizes wellness and caring for the person as a whole. Her
roach to healing and growth is centered on the mind-body connection and
rporates coaching, mindfulness, and other energy healing modalities
luding Reiki, breath work, EFT, human design, and more).

dy resides in San Diego, California and enjoys playing golf, doing pilates,
ding time in nature, and traveling to new destinations. She is also always
ning something new and excited to share her latest breakthroughs!

se visit **cindytsaimd.com** and connect with Cindy directly at
o@cindytsaimd.com to learn about her coaching and speaking services.

ow her latest updates on all the social media channels: @cindytsaimd

BONUS FREEBIE

Is it still hard to be kind to yourself sometimes?

Do you want to bring more love and compassion into your life?

Make sure to download my FREE guided
loving-kindness meditation!

Scan the following QR code to access NOW!

cindytsaimd.com/somuchbetterbookgift

Enjoy!

URGENT REQUEST

Thank you for reading my book!

If you found it helpful, can you please help me spread the word and tell at least two people who could benefit from it as well?

I really appreciate all of your feedback, and I love hearing what you have to say.

I need your input to make the next version of this book and future books better.

Please leave me a review on Amazon letting me know what you thought of the book.

I appreciate you so much!! Have a wonderful day!

All my best,
Cindy

Made in the USA
Las Vegas, NV
19 November 2022

59879321R00090